—— AMERICA'S
TEST KITC

Food Fun:
An Activity Book for Young Chefs

Library of Congress Cataloging-in-Publication Data

Names: America's Test Kitchen (Firm), author.
Title: Food fun : an activity book for young chefs : baking edition, 60+recipes, experiments, and games / America's Test Kitchen.
Description: Boston : America's Test Kitchen, [2021] | Includes index. | Audience: Ages 8-13 | Audience: Grades 4-6
Identifiers: LCCN 2021013724 (print) | LCCN 2021013725 (ebook) | ISBN 9781948703741 (paperback) | ISBN 9781948703758 (ebook)
Subjects: LCSH: Baking--Juvenile literature. | Games--Juvenile literature. | LCGFT: Cookbooks.
Classification: LCC TX763 .A45 2021 (print) | LCC TX763 (ebook) | DDC 641.81/5--dc23
LC record available at https://lccn.loc.gov/2021013724
LC ebook record available at https://lccn.loc.gov/2021013725

America's Test Kitchen
21 Drydock Avenue, Suite 210E
Boston, MA 02210

Printed in Canada
10 9 8 7 6 5 4 3 2 1
Distributed by Penguin Random House Publisher Services
Tel: 800.733.3000

Editor in Chief: Molly Birnbaum

Executive Food Editor: Suzannah McFerran

Executive Editor: Kristin Sargianis

Project Editor: Cheryl Redmond

Senior Editors: Ali Velez Alderfer, Afton Cyrus

Test Cooks: Cassandra Loftlin, Andrea Rivera Wawrzyn

Assistant Editors: Tess Berger, Katy O'Hara

Senior Science Research Editor: Paul Adams

Director of Marketing: Sally Calame

Digital Marketing Manager: Kelsey Hopper

Creative Director: John Torres

Associate Art Director: Gabi Homonoff

Staff Writer: Chad Chenail

Senior Manager, Publishing Operations: Taylor Argenzio

Lead Copy Editor: Rachel Schowalter

Copy Editors: Christine Campbell, April Poole

Chief Creative Officer: Jack Bishop

Executive Editorial Directors: Julia Collin Davison, Bridget Lancaster

Table of Contents

Introduction

Welcome to *Food Fun*! We created this baking activity book to help you learn how to bake; nerd out with science using food; and, most important, have fun. (Bonus: lots of delicious things to eat along the way!)

The recipes, experiments, and activities in this book are all kid tested and kid approved. This means that a group of more than 12,000 volunteer kid testers from around the country have baked or done every single one of the recipes, experiments, and activities in this book. They gave us suggestions for improvements and told us whether they'd make them again or recommend them to their friends.

This book is for you to write in, draw in, and make completely your own. Food is a wonderful way to get creative, to get messy, and to learn. You'll probably make some mistakes, but that's OK (they'll still be delicious). Be proud of all that you accomplish!

More than 12,000 kids helped create this book!

READY, SET, GO!

Understanding the Symbols in This Activity Book

To help you find the right recipe, experiment, or activity for you, we use a system of symbols to quickly show the type of cooking required:

 = requires use of knife

 = requires use of microwave

 = requires use of oven

 = no knives or heat required

Rate the Recipes

As you make each recipe, take notes (or make drawings) on the page. When you're finished, rate the recipe! Pick the emoji that best describes what you thought of the recipe and circle it or color it in.

RATE THE RECIPE

How to Read the Recipes in This Activity Book

Cooking from a recipe is actually a three-step process, and the recipes in this workbook are written to reflect that, with three distinct sections. Bonus: Each recipe is accompanied by additional information or an activity to grow your food and cooking knowledge.

Prepare Ingredients

Start with the list of ingredients and prepare them as directed. Wash fruits and vegetables. Measure ingredients, melt butter, and chop ingredients as needed. You can use small prep bowls to keep ingredients organized.

Gather Baking Equipment

Once all your ingredients are ready, put all the tools you will need to follow the recipe instructions on the counter.

Start Baking!

It's finally time to start baking. Any ingredients that need to be prepped at the last minute will have instructions within the recipe itself. Don't forget to have fun!

Food for Thought

Food and baking are about SO MUCH more than just what's happening in your pot or pan or bowl. Each recipe has a special "Food for Thought" section to inspire you to expand your knowledge and learn something new!

Kitchen Math

You can get carried away learning all the math behind measuring. Memorize the following rules and you will be all set.

3 teaspoons	=	1 tablespoon
16 tablespoons	=	1 cup
16 ounces	=	1 pound
2 cups	=	1 pint
4 cups	=	1 quart
4 quarts	=	1 gallon

Kitchen Safety Tips

- Wash your hands before cooking and after touching raw meat or eggs.
- Knives and stoves can be dangerous. Always ask for help if you're in doubt.
- Assume that anything on the stove or in the oven is hot. Use oven mitts.
- Never let ingredients you eat raw (such as berries) touch foods you will cook (such as eggs).
- Always turn off the stovetop and oven when you're done cooking.

How to Read the Experiments in This Activity Book

The goal of an experiment is to answer a question—such as "What's the difference between brown sugar and white sugar?" or "Why are there usually eggs in cake recipes?"—by gathering data and analyzing it. Like recipes, experiments follow a step-by-step process.

Materials

Start with the list of materials and prepare them as directed. Sometimes these materials are ingredients and kitchen equipment, but depending on the experiment, they might include other materials from around your house, such as craft materials or art supplies.

Make a Prediction

Before beginning an experiment, scientists use what they already know to make a prediction—an educated guess—about the answer to the question they're exploring. It helps them (and you!) think through the possibilities and record their ideas.

Observe Your Results

Now on to the testing! When you conduct your experiment following the steps in this book, carefully observe the results—there are designated spaces to write down (or draw pictures of) what you notice happening! Do your observations support or disprove your prediction? In this book, you'll use all your senses—sight, touch, taste, smell, and hearing—as you make your observations.

Understanding Your Results

After (and only after!) you've finished your experiment, read an explanation of the science behind your observations and learn more about the results we got when we did these experiments in the America's Test Kitchen Kids lab.

Decoding Kitchenspeak

Reading a recipe can sometimes feel like reading a different language. Here are some common words in many recipes and what they really mean.

PEEL: To remove the outer skin, rind, or layer from food, usually a piece of fruit or a vegetable. Often done with a vegetable peeler.

ZEST: To remove the flavorful colored outer peel from a citrus fruit such as a lemon, lime, or orange (the colored skin is called the zest). Does not include the bitter white layer (called the pith) under the zest.

CHOP: To cut food with a knife into small pieces. Chopped fine = ⅛- to ¼-inch pieces. Chopped = ¼- to ½-inch pieces. Chopped coarse = ½- to ¾-inch pieces. Use a ruler to understand the different sizes.

SLICE: To cut food with a knife into pieces with two flat sides, with the thickness dependent on the recipe instructions. For example, slicing a celery stalk.

GRATE: To cut food (often cheese) into very small, uniform pieces using a rasp grater or the small holes on a box grater.

STIR: To combine ingredients in a bowl or cooking vessel, often with a rubber spatula or wooden spoon.

TOSS: To gently combine ingredients with tongs or two forks and/or spoons in order to distribute the ingredients evenly. You toss salad in a bowl (you don't stir it).

MELT: To heat solid food (think butter) on the stovetop or in the microwave until it becomes a liquid.

SIMMER: To heat liquid until small bubbles gently break the surface at a variable and infrequent rate, as when cooking a soup.

BOIL: To heat liquid until large bubbles break the surface at a rapid and constant rate, as when cooking pasta.

Decoding Experimentspeak

Reading a science experiment can sometimes feel like reading a different language, too! Here are some common words in many experiments and what they really mean.

PREDICTION: An educated guess, based on your knowledge and experience, about what will happen in an experiment.

OBSERVATION: The act of careful watching, listening, touching, tasting, or smelling. When conducting experiments, scientists record their observations, usually by writing, drawing, or taking photos.

SUBJECT: When scientists conduct experiments, their "subjects" are the people whose reactions or responses they're studying.

VARIABLE: Something that can be changed. In experiments, scientists change at least one variable to observe what happens.

Here's an example: Scientists are studying whether the type of sugar affects the flavor and texture of cookies. They add brown sugar to one batch of cookies and white sugar to a second batch of cookies. The type of sugar is the variable.

CONTROLS: The variables that are not changed in an experiment.

For example, when the scientists are studying whether the type of sugar affects the flavor and texture of cookies, they use the same types and amounts of all cookie ingredients (except the sugar) and bake the cookies at the same temperature for the same amount of time.

BLIND: When the subjects of the experiment do not know what is being tested.

For example, subjects might wear a blindfold when tasting two different foods so that they can't see what they're eating or they might taste two batches of pasta, one cooked with salt and one cooked without salt, without being told what is different about them.

RESULTS: What happens in an experiment, usually a combination of the observations and measurements recorded and interpreted by scientists.

Sketch All these recipes were developed in our test kitchen. Draw what you think the test kitchen looks like in the box below!

FOOD FUN: AN ACTIVITY BOOK FOR YOUNG CHEFS

CHAPTER 1 Recipes and Make It Your Way Challenge

Sheet Pan French Toast

SERVES 4
TOTAL TIME 40 minutes

Prepare Ingredients

Vegetable oil spray

3 large eggs

1 tablespoon vanilla extract

2 teaspoons packed brown sugar

½ teaspoon ground cinnamon

¼ teaspoon salt

1 cup milk

2 tablespoons unsalted butter, melted and cooled

8 slices hearty white sandwich bread

Gather Baking Equipment

Rimmed baking sheet

Large bowl

Whisk

Oven mitts

Cooling rack

Start Baking!

1 Adjust 1 oven rack to lowest position and second rack 5 to 6 inches from broiler element. Heat oven to 425 degrees. Spray rimmed baking sheet well with vegetable oil spray.

2 In large bowl, whisk eggs, vanilla, brown sugar, cinnamon, and salt until well combined and sugar is dissolved, about 30 seconds. Add milk and melted butter and whisk until combined.

3 Pour egg mixture into greased baking sheet.

4 Place bread slices in 2 rows on baking sheet. Working quickly, flip each slice in same order you placed them on baking sheet. Let bread sit until slices absorb egg mixture, about 1 minute.

5 Place baking sheet in oven on lower rack and bake until bottoms of slices are golden brown, 10 to 15 minutes.

6 Use oven mitts to transfer baking sheet to upper rack and heat broiler (ask an adult for help). Broil until tops of slices are golden brown, 1 to 4 minutes (watch carefully to prevent burning!). Use oven mitts to remove baking sheet from oven and place on cooling rack (ask an adult for help). Serve.

Notes Use this space to write what you liked (or didn't like) about this recipe or draw a picture of what you made!

Food for Thought

When you add bread to the baking sheet full of egg mixture, the liquid seems to disappear! Where does it go? The bread soaks it up, or **absorbs** it. To see absorption in action, combine some water and a few drops of food coloring in a shallow dish, such as a pie plate. Place a slice of bread in the dish, let it sit for 1 minute, and then flip it over. What do you notice? Draw what the bread looks like in the space below.

The bread absorbs the colored water because it is porous, which means it's full of tiny holes and tunnels that lead to air pockets inside. When you place a slice of bread in liquid, such as water or the egg mixture in this recipe, the liquid moves into those holes and tunnels and fills up the empty air pockets. As this happens, the bread turns from light and dry to heavy and wet—and it changes color, too!

Spiced Applesauce Muffins

MAKES 12 muffins

TOTAL TIME 55 minutes, plus cooling time

Prepare Ingredients

Vegetable oil spray

¾ cup (3¾ ounces) all-purpose flour

¾ cup (4⅛ ounces) whole-wheat flour

1 teaspoon baking soda

½ teaspoon salt

⅔ cup (4⅔ ounces) sugar

½ teaspoon ground cinnamon

¼ teaspoon ground nutmeg

1 cup unsweetened applesauce

8 tablespoons unsalted butter, melted and cooled

¼ cup apple cider or apple juice

1 large egg

1 teaspoon vanilla extract

Gather Baking Equipment

12-cup muffin tin

3 bowls (1 large, 1 medium, 1 small)

Whisk

1-tablespoon measuring spoon

Rubber spatula

¼-cup dry measuring cup

Toothpick

Oven mitts

Cooling rack

Start Baking!

1 Adjust oven rack to middle position and heat oven to 375 degrees. Spray 12-cup muffin tin, including top, with vegetable oil spray.

2 In medium bowl, whisk together all-purpose flour, whole-wheat flour, baking soda, and salt.

3 In large bowl, whisk together sugar, cinnamon, and nutmeg. Transfer 2 tablespoons sugar mixture to small bowl and reserve for sprinkling.

4 Add applesauce, melted butter, cider, egg, and vanilla to remaining sugar mixture in large bowl and whisk until well combined.

5 Add flour mixture and use rubber spatula to gently stir until just combined and no dry flour is visible. Do not overmix.

6 Spray ¼-cup dry measuring cup with vegetable oil spray. Use greased measuring cup to divide batter evenly among muffin cups. Sprinkle reserved sugar mixture evenly over batter in each muffin cup.

7 Place muffin tin in oven. Bake until muffins are deep golden brown and toothpick inserted in center of 1 muffin comes out clean, 20 to 25 minutes.

8 Use oven mitts to remove muffin tin from oven and place on cooling rack (ask an adult for help). Let muffins cool in muffin tin for 15 minutes.

9 Using your fingertips, gently wiggle muffins to loosen from muffin tin and transfer to cooling rack. Let cool for at least 10 minutes before serving.

Food for Thought

These muffins include three spices—cinnamon, nutmeg, and vanilla—but they don't taste spicy, they taste sweet. Here is an important fact: Spiced is not the same as spicy.

Most spicy foods include chile peppers in some form, such as ground cayenne pepper, hot sauce, or crushed red pepper flakes. Chile peppers contain a chemical called capsaicin ("cap-SAY-sin") that makes us feel hotter than we actually are—that's why your mouth feels "on fire" when you eat something spicy.

Spiced foods, such as these muffins, are flavored using the power of spices. Most spices, including the ones in this recipe, aren't made from chile peppers but from other plants (learn more on page 71). And each spice is jam-packed with flavor. There are only 1¾ teaspoons of spices in this entire recipe—that's less than ¼ teaspoon per muffin—but you can definitely taste and smell the spices in every bite.

Explore your refrigerator, pantry, freezer, or local grocery store. What foods can you find that are spiced versus spicy? Jot them down in the spaces below.

Spiced	Spicy

Cherry, Almond, and Chocolate Chip Granola

 MAKES 5 cups

TOTAL TIME 1 hour and 10 minutes, plus cooling time

Prepare Ingredients

Vegetable oil spray

¼ cup vegetable oil

3 tablespoons maple syrup

2 tablespoons packed
light brown sugar

2 teaspoons vanilla extract

¼ teaspoon salt

2½ cups (7½ ounces) old-fashioned
rolled oats

1 cup (3½ ounces) sliced almonds

1 cup dried cherries

½ cup (3 ounces) semisweet
chocolate chips

Gather Baking Equipment

13-by-9-inch metal baking pan

2 bowls (1 large, 1 medium)

Rubber spatula

Oven mitts

Cooling rack

Butter knife

Start Baking!

1 Adjust oven rack to middle position
and heat oven to 325 degrees.
Spray inside bottom and sides of
13-by-9-inch metal baking pan with
vegetable oil spray.

2 In large bowl, combine oil, maple
syrup, brown sugar, vanilla, and
salt and use rubber spatula to stir
until well combined. Stir in oats and
almonds until combined.

3   Transfer oat mixture to greased baking pan and use rubber spatula to spread mixture into even layer. Use rubber spatula to press down firmly on oat mixture until mixture is very flat.

4   Place baking pan in oven. Bake until lightly browned, 35 to 40 minutes.

5   Use oven mitts to remove baking pan from oven and place on cooling rack (ask an adult for help). Let granola cool completely in pan, about 45 minutes.

6   Use butter knife to crack cooled granola into large pieces. Then, use your hands to break granola into bite-size pieces. Transfer granola to medium bowl. Use rubber spatula to stir in cherries and chocolate chips. Serve. (Granola can be stored in airtight container for up to 2 weeks.)

Food for Thought

It's important to measure all your ingredients carefully when you bake, and the best time to do that is before you begin the recipe. This is called mise en place ("MEEZ-on-plass"), which is a French cooking phrase that translates as "put in place" and means that everything is lined up and ready to go. Each ingredient goes into a small dish or bowl. It's a great way to make sure that nothing gets left out.

Once you've "mised" all your granola ingredients, and before you stir them all together, try lining them up in order, from the smallest amount to the largest. If two ingredients have the same measurement, put them next to one another.

In addition to looking at the ingredients to see which ones take up more space, it helps to remember how different measurements compare with each other: There are 3 teaspoons in 1 tablespoon, and there are 16 tablespoons in 1 cup.

 =

3 teaspoons = 1 tablespoon

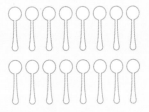 =

16 tablespoons = 1 cup

SEE PAGE 130 FOR ANSWER

Simple Cream Scones

 MAKES 8 scones
TOTAL TIME 40 minutes, plus cooling time

Prepare Ingredients

2 cups (10 ounces) all-purpose flour

3 tablespoons sugar

1 tablespoon baking powder

½ teaspoon salt

5 tablespoons unsalted butter, cut into ¼-inch pieces and chilled

1 cup heavy cream

Gather Baking Equipment

Rimmed baking sheet

Parchment paper

Food processor

Large bowl

Rubber spatula

Ruler

Bench scraper (or butter knife and spatula)

Oven mitts

Cooling rack

Start Baking!

1 Adjust oven rack to middle position and heat oven to 425 degrees. Line rimmed baking sheet with parchment paper.

2 Place flour, sugar, baking powder, and salt in food processor. Lock lid into place. Turn on processor and process mixture for 3 seconds. Stop processor.

3 Remove lid and sprinkle chilled butter over flour mixture. Lock lid back into place. Hold down pulse button for 1 second, then release. Repeat until mixture looks like coarse crumbs, about ten 1-second pulses. Remove lid and carefully remove processor blade (ask an adult for help).

4 Transfer flour-butter mixture to large bowl. Add cream and use rubber spatula to stir until just combined and no dry flour is visible. Do not overmix.

5 Transfer mixture to clean counter and use your hands to gather and press mixture until dough forms and holds together, 5 to 10 seconds. Pat dough into 8-inch circle, about ¾ inch thick.

6 Use bench scraper or butter knife to cut dough circle into 8 wedges. Use bench scraper or spatula to transfer scones to parchment-lined baking sheet.

7 Place baking sheet in oven. Bake until scones are light brown on top, 10 to 14 minutes.

8 Use oven mitts to remove baking sheet from oven and place on cooling rack (ask an adult for help). Let scones cool on baking sheet for 15 minutes.

9 Transfer scones directly to cooling rack. Let cool for 30 minutes before serving.

Notes Use this space to write what you liked (or didn't like) about this recipe or draw a picture of what you made!

Food for Thought

In step 6 of this recipe, you need to cut the circle of dough into eight equal pieces. Making all the pieces the same size helps them bake evenly. But how do you cut a circle into equal parts? You could just try cutting it into eight strips—but those wouldn't be **equal** parts.

The easiest way to get eight scones all the same size is to cut the circle of dough into eight equal wedges. Follow the steps below to practice.

Unequal parts

Cut the circle into two equal pieces. What fraction is each piece?

Now cut the circle into four equal pieces. What fraction is each piece?

Finally, cut the circle into eight equal pieces. What fraction is each piece?

SEE PAGE 130 FOR ANSWERS

Buffalo Chicken Lavash Flatbread

SERVES 2 to 4

TOTAL TIME 45 minutes

Prepare Ingredients

1 (12-by-9-inch) lavash

1 tablespoon extra-virgin olive oil

1 cup shredded cooked chicken (from rotisserie chicken or from leftovers)

2 tablespoons Frank's hot sauce (or other not-too-spicy hot sauce)

1 tablespoon unsalted butter, melted

¾ cup shredded Monterey Jack cheese (3 ounces)

½ cup baby spinach, chopped

Ranch dressing (optional)

Gather Baking Equipment

Rimmed baking sheet

Pastry brush

Oven mitts

Cooling rack

Medium bowl

Rubber spatula

Spatula

Cutting board

Chef's knife

Start Baking!

1 Adjust oven rack to lower-middle position and heat oven to 425 degrees. Lay lavash on rimmed baking sheet. Use pastry brush to paint both sides of lavash evenly with oil.

2 Place baking sheet in oven and bake until lavash is light golden brown, 3 to 4 minutes.

3 Use oven mitts to remove baking sheet from oven and place on cooling rack (ask an adult for help). Let lavash cool on baking sheet for 10 minutes.

4 While lavash cools, in medium bowl, combine chicken, hot sauce, and melted butter. Use rubber spatula to stir until chicken is well coated with sauce.

5 Sprinkle Monterey Jack evenly over cooled lavash. Spread chicken mixture evenly over cheese. Sprinkle with spinach.

6 Use oven mitts to return baking sheet to oven and bake until cheese is melted and chicken is warmed through, 4 to 6 minutes.

7 Use oven mitts to remove baking sheet from oven and place on cooling rack (ask an adult for help). Let lavash cool slightly on baking sheet, about 2 minutes. Use spatula to transfer lavash to cutting board (baking sheet will be hot). Cut into pieces and serve with ranch dressing (if using).

Notes Use this space to write what you liked (or didn't like) about this recipe or draw a picture of what you made!

Food for Thought

Lavash is an Armenian flatbread that is traditionally formed into an oval or rectangle. The lavash you buy in a supermarket is usually a rectangle. Do you know how to calculate the area of a rectangle? Area is the amount of surface in a given space—such as your flatbread. It is measured in square units, such as square inches or square meters.

To find out how many square inches make up the area of your flatbread, measure the length (the long side) and the width (the short side) and multiply those numbers. For a flatbread that measures 12 inches by 9 inches, you multiply 12 by 9, which equals 108 square inches.

Look around your kitchen for another object with a rectangular shape, like a cereal box or a cookbook. Grab a ruler and calculate the area of that rectangle.

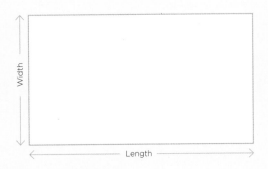

Measure the **length** of your rectangle: _____ inches

Measure the **width** of your rectangle: _____ inches

To calculate the area, multiply the **length** by the **width**.

_____ x _____ = _____ square inches

Length   Width   Area

Ham and Cheese Sliders

  SERVES 2

TOTAL TIME 25 minutes

Prepare Ingredients

4 teaspoons yellow mustard

4 potato dinner rolls, sliced open

4 slices deli ham

8 dill pickle chips

2 slices deli cheddar cheese, cut in half

Gather Baking Equipment

Rimmed baking sheet

Parchment paper

Butter knife

Oven mitts

Cooling rack

Spatula

2 serving plates

Start Baking!

1 Adjust oven rack to middle position and heat oven to 400 degrees. Line rimmed baking sheet with parchment paper.

2 Use butter knife to spread mustard evenly over insides of rolls.

3 Layer 1 slice ham, 2 pickle chips, and ½ slice cheddar into each roll and press down gently (you should have 4 sliders).

4 Place sliders on parchment-lined baking sheet. Place baking sheet in oven and bake until cheese has melted and rolls are crisp, about 5 minutes.

5 Use oven mitts to remove baking sheet from oven and place on cooling rack (ask an adult for help). Use spatula to carefully transfer sliders to 2 serving plates (baking sheet will be hot). Serve.

Notes Use this space to write what you liked (or didn't like) about this recipe or draw a picture of what you made!

Food for Thought

One important skill that chefs use is being able to scale a recipe up or down. Scaling a recipe means changing the ingredient amounts so that it can serve more people or fewer people. This recipe makes four sliders, which is enough to serve two people (each person eats two sliders). Use your multiplication and division skills to figure out how you would scale this recipe to serve a crowd (or enjoy for a solo lunch).

* If you want to make enough sliders for just 1 person, how many sliders will you need to make? How many teaspoons of yellow mustard will you need?

* If you want to make enough sliders for 8 people, how many dill pickle chips will you need?

* If there are 4 people in your family, and they all want sliders for lunch, how many sliders will you need to make? How many slices of ham will you need? How many slices of cheese?

SEE PAGE 130 FOR ANSWERS

Baked Macaroni and Cheese

 SERVES 4 to 6

TOTAL TIME 1 hour, plus cooling time

Make sure to use thinly sliced American cheese from the deli section of your grocery store in this recipe, not individually wrapped cheese "singles"—they are made from different ingredients.

Prepare Ingredients

2 cups (8 ounces) elbow macaroni

1 cup shredded mild cheddar cheese (4 ounces)

8–10 thin slices deli American cheese, torn into small pieces (4 ounces)

1 tablespoon cornstarch

½ teaspoon dry mustard

½ teaspoon salt

2 cups water

1 cup milk

½ cup frozen peas (optional)

Gather Baking Equipment

8-inch square baking dish

Rubber spatula

Aluminum foil

Oven mitts

Cooling rack

Start Baking!

1 Adjust oven rack to middle position and heat oven to 400 degrees. In 8-inch square baking dish, use rubber spatula to toss together macaroni, cheddar, American cheese, cornstarch, mustard, and salt.

2 Pour water and milk over macaroni mixture. Cover baking dish with aluminum foil.

3 Place baking dish in oven. Bake until macaroni is tender, about 35 minutes.

4 Use oven mitts to remove baking dish from oven and place on cooling rack (ask an adult for help).

5 Use oven mitts to uncover dish and use rubber spatula to carefully stir mixture until it looks creamy (ask an adult for help; dish will be hot), about 1 minute. Stir in peas (if using). Let cool for 10 minutes. Stir again before serving.

Food for Thought

Aluminum foil is actually a very thin, flexible sheet of a type of metal called . . . aluminum! In this recipe, you cover the baking dish tightly with a piece of aluminum foil before you put the macaroni and cheese in the oven. As the mac and cheese heats up, some of the water in the recipe turns into hot steam. The aluminum foil traps that steam inside the baking dish, where it helps cook the pasta and melt the cheese—and gives you a gooey, creamy finished result. You can see the steam escape when you remove the aluminum foil in step 5.

One interesting fact about aluminum foil is that it's great at conducting heat—that means heat moves into the foil very quickly, making it hot. It also means heat leaves the foil very quickly, cooling it down. (Ask an adult to let you feel the aluminum foil after you uncover the baking dish in step 5 of this recipe—even though the foil has been out of the oven for only a few minutes, it should be quite cool.)

Here's another way you can feel this in action: Cut or tear a strip of aluminum foil about 2 inches wide and 8 inches long. Fill a mug or drinking glass with hot tap water. Place one end of the strip in the water for 1 minute. Remove the foil strip from the water and hold one end in each hand. Count how many seconds it takes for the end that was in hot water to cool down and feel the same as the other end.

Record your observations in the space below.

Fancy Fish in Foil

SERVES 4

TOTAL TIME 35 minutes

Prepare Ingredients

1 teaspoon fresh thyme leaves

½ teaspoon grated lemon zest, zested from ½ lemon, plus lemon wedges for serving

½ teaspoon salt

⅛ teaspoon pepper

4 (6-ounce) skinless cod fillets, 1 to 1½ inches thick

4 tablespoons unsalted butter, cut into 4 pieces

Gather Baking Equipment

Aluminum foil

Small bowl

Spoon

Rimmed baking sheet

Instant-read thermometer

Oven mitts

Cooling rack

4 serving plates

Start Baking!

1 Adjust oven rack to middle position and heat oven to 450 degrees. Cut 4 large pieces of aluminum foil.

2 In small bowl, add thyme, lemon zest, salt, and pepper and stir with spoon to combine. Place 1 cod fillet on 1 side of each piece of foil. Sprinkle thyme mixture evenly over fillets and top with butter. Wash your hands.

3 Fold empty side of foil over cod fillet. Fold up edges of foil and pinch together to create sealed packet. Transfer packets to rimmed baking sheet.

4 Place baking sheet in oven. Bake until cod registers 140 degrees on instant-read thermometer, 12 to 15 minutes.

5 Use oven mitts to remove baking sheet from oven and place on cooling rack (ask an adult for help). Transfer packets to 4 serving plates and carefully open. Serve with lemon wedges.

Notes
Use this space to write what you liked (or didn't like) about this recipe or draw a picture of what you made!

Food for Thought

The name of this recipe is "Fancy Fish in Foil," which is an example of alliteration ("uh-lit-er-RAY-shun"). Alliteration is when the first consonant sounds in words are repeated in neighboring words. In this case, the three main words in the recipe name— Fancy Fish in Foil—start with the letter "F" and the sound "fff."

Can you think of alliterative names for other recipes you like to cook or foods you like to eat? First, think of the name of a dish (such as "meatballs"). Then, think of adjectives (describing words) that start with those same beginning consonant sounds ("mmm" like "marvelous" or "magnificent"). See how many words with similar consonant sounds you can string together to make your recipe name—two, three, even four? Write your recipe names in the spaces at the right.

Practically Perfect Pepperoni Pizza

Cake Pan Pizza

SERVES 4 to 6 (Makes two 9-inch pizzas)
TOTAL TIME 1 hour

Prepare Ingredients

2 tablespoons extra-virgin olive oil

1 pound pizza dough

½ cup pizza sauce or marinara sauce

1 cup shredded mozzarella cheese
(4 ounces)

2 tablespoons grated
Parmesan cheese (¼ ounce)

Gather Baking Equipment

2 dark-colored 9-inch round metal
cake pans

Plastic wrap

Spoon

Oven mitts

Cooling rack

Spatula

Cutting board

Chef's knife

Start Baking!

1 Adjust oven rack to middle position
and heat oven to 450 degrees. Divide
oil evenly between 2 dark-colored
9-inch round metal cake pans. Use
your fingers to spread oil evenly over
bottoms and sides of pans.

2 Divide dough in half. Pat and flatten
each piece of dough into circle. Place
1 dough circle in each cake pan and
turn to coat with oil.

3 Cover cake pans loosely with plastic
wrap. Let dough rise on counter until
slightly puffy, about 30 minutes.

4 When dough is ready, gently push
and stretch dough to cover bottoms
of pans (all the way to edges).

5 Spoon pizza sauce evenly over
both dough circles and use back
of spoon to spread into even layer,
leaving ½-inch border. Sprinkle each
pizza evenly with mozzarella and
Parmesan.

6 Place cake pans in oven. Bake pizzas until cheese is beginning to brown, 10 to 15 minutes.

7 Use oven mitts to remove cake pans from oven and place on cooling rack (ask an adult for help). Let pizzas cool in pans for 5 minutes. Use spatula to transfer pizzas to cutting board (pans will be hot). Cut into wedges and serve.

Notes Use this space to write what you liked (or didn't like) about this recipe or draw a picture of what you made!

Food for Thought

We think this pizza is so good that it deserves to have a story written about it. A comic strip is a sequence of boxes (called panels) with drawings—and sometimes words—that tells a story. It can be silly or serious. Every story, whether it is short or long, has three parts: the beginning, the middle, and the end. This comic has a beginning and middle, but no end—yet! How do you think this story turns out? Write and draw your ending in the blank panel.

ON PAGE 128 YOU CAN CREATE YOUR OWN COMIC STRIP STORY, FROM BEGINNING TO END.

Firecracker Hot Dogs

SERVES **8**

TOTAL TIME **45 minutes, plus cooling time**

Serve with ketchup and/or mustard.

Prepare Ingredients

Vegetable oil spray

8 hot dogs

1 can biscuit dough

1 large egg, lightly beaten

1 tablespoon sesame seeds

Gather Baking Equipment

Rimmed baking sheet

Parchment paper

8 wooden skewers

Ruler

Chef's knife (or bench scraper)

Pastry brush

Oven mitts

Cooling rack

Start Baking!

1 Adjust oven rack to middle position and heat oven to 375 degrees. Line rimmed baking sheet with parchment paper. Spray parchment lightly with vegetable oil spray.

2 Carefully push 1 wooden skewer lengthwise (the long way) through center of each hot dog.

3 Use your hands to pat and stretch 1 biscuit dough round into oval, about 8 inches long. Cut oval in half lengthwise (the long way) to make 2 strips. Repeat stretching and cutting with 3 additional biscuit dough rounds (you should have 8 strips of dough).

4 Starting from top, wrap 1 dough strip around each hot dog in spiral, leaving gaps in spiral as you wrap. Place on parchment-lined baking sheet, tucking ends of dough strips underneath hot dogs.

5 Use pastry brush to brush tops of dough strips with egg. Sprinkle sesame seeds over top.

6 Place baking sheet in oven. Bake until biscuit strips are golden brown, about 15 minutes.

7 Use oven mitts to remove baking sheet from oven and place on cooling rack (ask an adult for help). Let hot dogs cool on baking sheet for 10 minutes. Serve.

Notes Use this space to write what you liked (or didn't like) about this recipe or draw a picture of what you made!

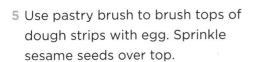
Food for Thought

To turn plain hot dogs into fancy firecrackers, you wrap a long strip of biscuit dough around each hot dog, making a spiral. You can form the spiral in two directions: clockwise or counterclockwise. Can you move in both of those directions?

Set a chair (or another object) in the middle of the floor, point at the chair with your right hand, and walk around it in a circle so that it is always on your right side. You are moving clockwise, the same way that the hands move around a clock. Now point to the chair with your left hand and walk around it, keeping the chair on your left side; you are moving counterclockwise, the opposite of the way the hands move around a clock.

Draw an arrow moving clockwise around this circle.

Draw an arrow moving counterclockwise around this circle.

In step 4 of this recipe, try wrapping four hot dogs with a clockwise dough spiral and four hot dogs with a counterclockwise dough spiral. Start by holding the skewered hot dog so that you're looking down at the top of the hot dog. After you get it started you can hold the hot dog flat if you like. Do the finished Firecracker Hot Dogs look different depending on whether you wrapped the dough around clockwise or counterclockwise? How so?

SEE PAGE 130 FOR ANSWER

Oatmeal-Raisin Cookies

  MAKES 12 cookies
TOTAL TIME 40 minutes, plus cooling time

For these cookies, we had the best luck using Quaker old-fashioned rolled oats. Don't use quick, instant, or extra-thick rolled oats in this recipe.

Prepare Ingredients

½ cup (2½ ounces) all-purpose flour

½ teaspoon salt

¼ teaspoon baking soda

½ cup packed (3½ ounces) light brown sugar

¼ cup vegetable oil

2 tablespoons unsalted butter, melted and cooled

⅛ teaspoon ground cinnamon

1 large egg

½ teaspoon vanilla extract

1½ cups (4½ ounces) old-fashioned rolled oats

¼ cup raisins

Gather Baking Equipment

Rimmed baking sheet

Parchment paper

2 bowls (1 large, 1 medium)

Whisk

Rubber spatula

1-tablespoon measuring spoon

Ruler

Oven mitts

Cooling rack

Spatula

Start Baking!

1 Adjust oven rack to middle position and heat oven to 375 degrees. Line rimmed baking sheet with parchment paper.

2 In medium bowl, whisk together flour, salt, and baking soda.

3 In large bowl, whisk together brown sugar, oil, melted butter, and cinnamon. Add egg and vanilla and whisk until mixture is smooth.

4 Add flour mixture to brown sugar mixture and use rubber spatula to stir until fully combined, about 1 minute. Add oats and raisins and stir until evenly distributed.

5 Use 1-tablespoon measuring spoon to drop dough onto parchment-lined baking sheet in 12 mounds (about 2 heaping tablespoons each). Leave space between mounds. Wet your hand lightly, then use your damp hand to gently flatten each mound into 2-inch-wide circle.

6 Place baking sheet in oven. Bake cookies until edges are set and lightly browned but centers are still soft, 8 to 10 minutes.

7 Use oven mitts to remove baking sheet from oven and place on cooling rack (ask an adult for help). Let cookies cool on baking sheet for 10 minutes.

8 Use spatula to transfer cookies directly to cooling rack. Let cool completely, about 15 minutes. Serve.

Notes Use this space to write what you liked (or didn't like) about this recipe or draw a picture of what you made!

Food for Thought

Oats come from a type of grass plant. (No, not the grass you see on a baseball diamond—this grass plant can grow to be 5 feet tall!) The grass produces seeds with hard outer shells, called hulls. Once the hull is removed, what's left is called a groat (think of it as a **gr**ain of **oat**).

Manufacturers use machines to process the groats in different ways, which turn into the different types of oats, such as steel-cut oats, rolled oats (used in this recipe), and instant oats. What kinds of oats do you have in your kitchen? See what you can find and pour a small amount of each kind into a dish. What does each variety look like up close? (Use a magnifying glass if you have one.) How are they similar or different? Do you have any guesses about how each type is made?

Steel-Cut Oats: Groats are sliced into three or four pieces using steel blades, hence the name. They have a coarse, chunky texture.

Stone-Ground Oats: Also called Scottish oats, these are similar to steel-cut oats, but the groats are ground into small pieces between flat, heavy milling stones.

Old-Fashioned or Rolled Oats: Groats are steamed and then rolled flat by metal rollers, which gives them their flat, oval shape.

Quick Oats: Steel-cut oats are steamed and then rolled flat until they're even thinner than old-fashioned oats.

Instant Oats: Groats are first cut into very, very small pieces. Then they're cooked and rolled flat before they're dried.

Simple Sugar Cookies

  MAKES 12 cookies

TOTAL TIME 40 minutes, plus cooling time

Prepare Ingredients

1 cup (5 ounces) all-purpose flour

¼ teaspoon baking soda

¼ teaspoon salt

¾ cup (5¼ ounces) sugar

4 tablespoons unsalted butter, melted

1 large egg

1 teaspoon vanilla extract

Gather Baking Equipment

Rimmed baking sheet

Parchment paper

2 bowls (1 large, 1 medium)

Whisk

Rubber spatula

1-tablespoon measuring spoon

Oven mitts

Cooling rack

Start Baking!

1 Adjust oven rack to middle position and heat oven to 325 degrees. Line rimmed baking sheet with parchment paper.

2 In medium bowl, whisk together flour, baking soda, and salt.

3 In large bowl, whisk sugar and melted butter until smooth. Add egg and vanilla and whisk until well combined.

4 Add flour mixture to sugar mixture and use rubber spatula to stir until no dry flour is visible and soft dough forms.

5 Use your hands to roll dough into 12 balls (about 1 heaping tablespoon each). Place dough balls on parchment-lined baking sheet, leaving space between balls. Use your hand to gently flatten each dough ball.

6 Place baking sheet in oven. Bake cookies until edges are just set and centers are still soft, 11 to 13 minutes.

7 Use oven mitts to remove baking sheet from oven and place on cooling rack (ask an adult for help). Let cookies cool completely on baking sheet, about 30 minutes. Serve.

Notes Use this space to write what you liked (or didn't like) about this recipe or draw a picture of what you made!

Food for Thought

An acrostic ("uh-CROSS-tick") is a kind of poem in which the first letter of each line spells out a word or phrase. That word or phrase is the subject of the poem. The lines don't need to rhyme, and they can be as long or as short as you like. Take a look at the example below, and then make up your own acrostic by filling in the lines next to the word "cookie" (spelled out vertically below on the right). You can use these sugar cookies for inspiration: As you munch on one, think about how it tastes, what it looks like, or how you made it. Or write an acrostic poem about your favorite kind of cookie instead. For an extra challenge, try to rhyme each line.

Chewy and sweet   **C** _____

Outstanding with milk   **O** _____

Offer them to friends   **O** _____

Keep a few for me   **K** _____

If only I had more   **I** _____

Eager to make them again   **E** _____

ON PAGE 126 YOU CAN LEARN MORE ABOUT ACROSTIC POEMS!

Buttery Walnut Cookies

MAKES 24 cookies

TOTAL TIME 50 minutes, plus cooling time

Prepare Ingredients

1 cup (4 ounces) walnuts

1 cup (5 ounces) all-purpose flour

½ teaspoon salt

8 tablespoons unsalted butter, cut into 8 pieces and softened

¼ cup (1¾ ounces) sugar

¾ teaspoon vanilla extract

¾ cup (3 ounces) confectioners' (powdered) sugar

Gather Baking Equipment

Rimmed baking sheet

Parchment paper

Large zipper-lock plastic bag

Rolling pin

Medium bowl

Whisk

Shallow dish

Electric mixer (stand mixer with paddle attachment or handheld mixer and large bowl)

Rubber spatula

1-tablespoon measuring spoon

Oven mitts

Cooling rack

Start Baking!

1 Adjust oven rack to middle position and heat oven to 325 degrees. Line rimmed baking sheet with parchment paper.

2 Place walnuts in large zipper-lock plastic bag and seal, removing as much air as possible from bag. Use rolling pin to gently pound walnuts into very small pieces.

3 In medium bowl, whisk together pounded walnuts, flour, and salt.

4 Add softened butter and sugar to bowl of stand mixer (or large bowl if using handheld mixer). If using stand mixer, lock bowl into place and attach paddle. Start mixer on medium-high speed and beat until pale and fluffy, 3 to 4 minutes. Stop mixer and use rubber spatula to scrape down bowl.

5 Add vanilla and flour mixture. Start mixer on low speed and mix until combined, about 45 seconds. Stop mixer.

6 Remove bowl from stand mixer, if using. Use rubber spatula to scrape down bowl and stir in any remaining dry flour.

7 Use your hands to roll dough into 24 balls (about 1 tablespoon each). Place dough balls on parchment-lined baking sheet, leaving space between balls.

8 Place baking sheet in oven. Bake cookies until tops are pale golden and bottoms are just beginning to brown, about 18 minutes.

9 Use oven mitts to remove baking sheet from oven and place on cooling rack (ask an adult for help). Let cookies cool completely on baking sheet, about 20 minutes.

10 Set 1 cookie aside (see "Food for Thought"). Spread confectioners' sugar in shallow dish. Working with 4 cookies at a time, roll cookies in confectioners' sugar to coat. Just before serving, reroll cookies in confectioners' sugar a second time.

Notes Use this space to write what you liked (or didn't like) about this recipe or draw a picture of what you made!

Food for Thought

These cookies get rolled in confectioners' (powdered) sugar not once, but twice—right after they've cooled and a second time right before serving. Why do you think this recipe calls for rolling the cookies in confectioners' sugar and not granulated sugar?

To find out, before you follow step 10 of this recipe, set aside one cookie. Roll the remaining cookies in confectioners' sugar as directed. Add 1 tablespoon of granulated sugar to a small plate and roll the reserved cookie in it—what do you notice about how each type of sugar sticks to the cookies? Does one kind do a better job of coating the cookies? Why do you think that is?

Draw your observations here.

Granulated sugar, often just called "sugar," is made from sugarcane or beets and is in the form of tiny, irregularly shaped crystals. Confectioners' (powdered) sugar is granulated sugar that's ground to a very fine powder and mixed with a little bit of cornstarch to stop it from clumping. The fine, powdery texture of confectioners' sugar does a better job of coating and sticking to the cookie than the (relatively) larger grains of the granulated sugar.

Spiced Sesame Cookies

MAKES 24 cookies
TOTAL TIME 1 hour, plus cooling time

Ghee is a type of clarified butter that's used in Indian and Middle Eastern cooking. You can find it in the international section of many grocery stores or with cooking oils. You can also substitute butter.

Prepare Ingredients

1½ cups (7½ ounces) all-purpose flour

½ cup (2 ounces) confectioners' (powdered) sugar, plus extra for dusting

2 tablespoons sesame seeds, toasted

1 teaspoon ground cinnamon

½ teaspoon baking powder

⅛ teaspoon salt

⅔ cup ghee, melted, or 10 tablespoons unsalted butter, melted

⅓ cup milk

1 teaspoon vanilla extract

Gather Baking Equipment

Rimmed baking sheet

Parchment paper

Large bowl

Whisk

Rubber spatula

1-tablespoon measuring spoon

Fork

Oven mitts

Cooling rack

Fine-mesh strainer

Start Baking!

1 Adjust oven rack to middle position and heat oven to 350 degrees. Line baking sheet with parchment paper.

2 In large bowl, whisk together flour, confectioners' sugar, sesame seeds, cinnamon, baking powder, and salt.

3 Add melted ghee, milk, and vanilla to flour mixture. Use rubber spatula to stir until no dry flour is visible and soft dough forms.

4 Use your hands to roll dough into 24 balls (about 1 level tablespoon each). Place dough balls on parchment-lined baking sheet, leaving space between balls.

5 Use your hands to gently flatten each dough ball. Use side of fork to firmly press diamond crosshatch pattern in each cookie.

6 Place baking sheet in oven. Bake cookies until light golden brown, 20 to 24 minutes.

7 Use oven mitts to remove baking sheet from oven and place on cooling rack (ask an adult for help). Let cookies cool completely on baking sheet, about 30 minutes.

8 In fine-mesh strainer, add 1 to 2 tablespoons confectioners' sugar. Hold strainer over cookies and tap side of strainer to dust lightly with sugar. Serve.

Food for Thought

The Muslim holiday of Eid al-Fitr ("eed ul-FIT-ter") celebrates the end of the month of Ramadan. During Ramadan, Muslims fast during the day, which means they don't eat or drink. (They do eat before dawn and after the sun sets.) Eid al-Fitr means "Festival of Breaking the Fast" in Arabic, and families celebrate by visiting friends and neighbors and enjoying lots of foods, including these cookies. On Eid, people greet one another by saying "Eid Mubarak!" Mubarak ("moo-BAH-rahk") means "blessed" in Arabic.

For Muslims, part of Eid al-Fitr is giving thanks for the blessings that Allah (God) has bestowed upon them. What are some things that you are thankful for?

Many Muslims also celebrate the holiday by donating food (or money to buy food) to those in need. What are some kind or generous things that you could do for others this week or this month? It might be for someone in your household, in your community, or across the world.

Blondies

MAKES 16 blondies
TOTAL TIME 50 minutes, plus 2 hours cooling time

Prepare Ingredients

Vegetable oil spray

1 cup (5 ounces) all-purpose flour

¼ teaspoon baking powder

¼ teaspoon salt

1 cup packed (7 ounces) light brown sugar

8 tablespoons unsalted butter, melted

1 large egg

1 teaspoon vanilla extract

⅔ cup (2⅔ ounces) pecans, chopped

½ cup (3 ounces) chocolate chips

Gather Baking Equipment

Aluminum foil	Rubber spatula
8-inch square metal baking pan	Oven mitts
	Cooling rack
2 bowls (1 large, 1 medium)	Cutting board
Whisk	Chef's knife

Start Baking!

1 Adjust oven rack to middle position and heat oven to 350 degrees. Fold 2 long sheets of aluminum foil so each one is 8 inches wide. Lay sheets of foil in 8-inch square metal baking pan so sheets are perpendicular to each other. Let extra foil hang over edges of pan. Push foil into corners and up sides of pan, smoothing foil so it rests against pan. Spray foil with vegetable oil spray.

2 In medium bowl, whisk together flour, baking powder, and salt.

3 In large bowl, whisk brown sugar and melted butter until combined. Add egg and vanilla and whisk until combined.

4 Add flour mixture and use rubber spatula to stir until no dry flour remains. Add pecans and chocolate chips and stir to combine. Use rubber spatula to scrape batter into foil-lined baking pan and smooth top.

5 Place baking pan in oven. Bake until top is shiny and cracked and feels firm to touch, 25 to 27 minutes.

6 Use oven mitts to remove baking pan from oven and place on cooling rack (ask an adult for help). Let blondies cool completely in pan, about 2 hours.

7 Use foil to carefully lift blondies out of baking pan and transfer to cutting board. Cut into squares and serve.

Notes Use this space to write what you liked (or didn't like) about this recipe or draw a picture of what you made!

Food for Thought

While the blondies bake, sink your teeth into these math problems.

- This recipe makes 16 blondies. If you eat 2 blondies every day, how many days will this batch of blondies last?

- Imagine you bring your blondies to a bake sale and charge customers $0.75 for 1 blondie. If you sell all 16 blondies, how much money will you earn?

- One blondie recipe uses ½ cup of chocolate chips. If you wanted to make this recipe 5 times, how many cups of chocolate chips would you need in total?

SEE PAGE 130 FOR ANSWERS

Easy Chocolate Snack Cake

SERVES 12

TOTAL TIME 1 hour and 10 minutes, plus 2 hours cooling time

Prepare Ingredients

Vegetable oil spray

1½ cups (7½ ounces) all-purpose flour

1 cup (7 ounces) sugar

½ teaspoon baking soda

¼ teaspoon salt

½ cup (1½ ounces) Dutch-processed cocoa powder

⅓ cup (2 ounces) chocolate chips

1 cup water

⅔ cup mayonnaise

1 large egg

2 teaspoons vanilla extract

Confectioners' (powdered) sugar

Gather Baking Equipment

8-inch square metal baking pan

8-inch square piece of parchment paper

2 bowls (1 large, 1 medium)

Whisk

Liquid measuring cup

Oven mitts

Rubber spatula

Toothpick

Cooling rack

Fine-mesh strainer

Cutting board

Chef's knife

Start Baking!

1 Adjust oven rack to middle position and heat oven to 350 degrees. Spray inside bottom and sides of 8-inch square metal baking pan with vegetable oil spray. Line bottom of greased baking pan with 8-inch square piece of parchment paper.

2 In medium bowl, whisk together flour, sugar, baking soda, and salt. In large bowl, combine cocoa and chocolate chips.

3 Heat water in liquid measuring cup in microwave until hot and steaming, 1 to 2 minutes. Use oven mitts to remove measuring cup from microwave. Carefully pour water over chocolate mixture and whisk until smooth. Let mixture cool for 10 minutes.

4 Add mayonnaise, egg, and vanilla to cooled chocolate mixture and whisk until combined. Add flour mixture and use rubber spatula to stir until just combined and no dry flour remains.

5 Use rubber spatula to scrape batter into parchment-lined baking pan and smooth top (make sure to spread batter into corners to create even layer).

6 Place baking pan in oven. Bake until toothpick inserted in center of cake comes out clean, 34 to 38 minutes.

7 Use oven mitts to remove baking pan from oven and place on cooling rack (ask an adult for help). Let cake cool completely in pan, about 2 hours.

8 Remove cake from baking pan. Carefully peel parchment away from cake and discard. In fine-mesh strainer, add 1 to 2 tablespoons confectioners' sugar. Hold strainer over cake and tap side of strainer to dust lightly with sugar. Cut cake into pieces and serve.

Food for Thought

This cake includes a surprising ingredient: mayonnaise! In what kinds of recipes or foods do you usually eat mayonnaise? What do you think mayonnaise is doing in this cake recipe? (Spoiler: You won't be able to taste the mayo in your finished cake.)

Take a look at the ingredient list on the jar of mayonnaise you used when making your cake. Do you see any ingredients that might be at home in a recipe for cake? Check out the recipes for Carrot Snack Cake (page 44) and Birthday Cupcakes (page 46) for some hints! Write the ingredients here.

Two ingredients you'll find in lots of cake recipes—eggs and oil—are key ingredients in mayonnaise. Using mayonnaise gets them into your cake, even if you don't have eggs and oil on hand! This trick dates back to the Great Depression in the 1920s and 1930s, when people didn't always have eggs and oil in their pantries, so when they were baking they made do by using something they did have on hand: mayonnaise. The results were moist, cakey, and delicious!

Carrot Snack Cake

SERVES 12

TOTAL TIME 1 hour and 10 minutes, plus 1½ hours cooling time

Prepare Ingredients

Vegetable oil spray

1¼ cups (6¼ ounces) all-purpose flour

1½ teaspoons baking powder

½ teaspoon baking soda

½ teaspoon ground cinnamon

¼ teaspoon ground nutmeg

¼ teaspoon salt

¾ cup (5¼ ounces) sugar

⅔ cup vegetable oil

¼ cup packed (1¾ ounces) light brown sugar

2 large eggs

1 teaspoon vanilla extract

8 ounces carrots (about 3 medium), peeled and shredded

Gather Baking Equipment

8-inch square metal baking pan

8-inch square piece of parchment paper

2 bowls (1 large, 1 medium)

Whisk

Rubber spatula

Toothpick

Oven mitts

Cooling rack

Cutting board

Chef's knife

Start Baking!

1 Adjust oven rack to middle position and heat oven to 350 degrees. Spray inside bottom and sides of 8-inch square metal baking pan with vegetable oil spray. Line bottom of baking pan with 8-inch square piece of parchment paper.

2 In medium bowl, whisk together flour, baking powder, baking soda, cinnamon, nutmeg, and salt.

3 In large bowl, whisk sugar, oil, brown sugar, eggs, and vanilla until fully combined, about 1 minute.

4 Add flour mixture to sugar mixture and use rubber spatula to stir until just combined and no dry flour is visible. Add carrots to batter and stir until well combined.

5 Use rubber spatula to scrape batter into parchment-lined baking pan and smooth top (make sure to spread batter into corners to create even layer).

6 Place baking pan in oven. Bake until cake is golden brown and toothpick inserted in center comes out clean, 35 to 40 minutes.

7 Use oven mitts to remove baking pan from oven and place on cooling rack (ask an adult for help). Let cake cool completely in pan, about 1½ hours.

8 Remove cake from baking pan. Carefully peel parchment away from cake and discard. Cut cake into pieces and serve.

Notes Use this space to write what you liked (or didn't like) about this recipe or draw a picture of what you made!

Food for Thought

What color do you think of when you think of carrots? Carrots can come in different colors, such as purple and yellow, but most often we think of them as being bright orange. That bright orange color comes from a family of plant pigments (or colors) called carotenoids. Carotenoids give fruits and vegetables red, orange, and yellow colors. Other pigments turn fruits and vegetables other colors. Chlorophylls are responsible for the green color in green fruits and vegetables, and anthocyanins contribute to red, purple, and blue colors. But these pigments aren't just for show; they also give fruits and vegetables a nutritious punch. For instance, the beta-carotene found in carrots converts into vitamin A when you eat it. Vitamin A helps keep your eyes healthy.

There are fruits and veggies in every color of the rainbow: red, orange, yellow, green, blue, and purple. See how many you can think of for each color. If you like, have a contest with your friends and family: Set a timer for 2 minutes for each color and see who can write down the most fruits and vegetables in that color before the time is up.

Birthday Cupcakes

 MAKES 12 cupcakes

TOTAL TIME 40 minutes, plus 1¼ hours cooling time

Prepare Ingredients

1¾ cups (8¾ ounces) all-purpose flour

1 cup (7 ounces) sugar

1½ teaspoons baking powder

¾ teaspoon salt

12 tablespoons unsalted butter, cut into 12 pieces and softened

3 large eggs

¾ cup milk

1½ teaspoons vanilla extract

Vanilla Frosting (page 96)

Gather Baking Equipment

12-cup muffin tin

12 paper cupcake liners

Large bowl

Whisk

Electric mixer

Rubber spatula

⅓-cup dry measuring cup

Toothpick

Oven mitts

Cooling rack

Small icing spatula or spoon

Start Baking!

1 Adjust oven rack to middle position and heat oven to 350 degrees. Line 12-cup muffin tin with 12 paper liners.

2 In large bowl, whisk together flour, sugar, baking powder, and salt.

3 Add softened butter, 1 piece at a time, and beat with electric mixer on low speed until mixture resembles coarse sand, about 1 minute.

4 Add eggs, one at a time, and beat until combined.

5 Add milk and vanilla; increase speed to medium; and beat until light and fluffy and no lumps remain, about 2 minutes.

6 Use ⅓-cup dry measuring cup to divide batter evenly among muffin tin cups (use rubber spatula to scrape batter from measuring cup if needed).

7 Place muffin tin in oven. Bake cupcakes until toothpick inserted in center of 1 cupcake comes out clean, about 20 minutes.

8 Use oven mitts to remove muffin tin from oven and place on cooling rack (ask an adult for help). Let cupcakes cool in muffin tin for 15 minutes.

9 Remove cupcakes from muffin tin and transfer to cooling rack. Let cupcakes cool completely, about 1 hour.

10 Use small icing spatula or spoon to spread frosting over cupcakes. Serve.

Notes Use this space to write what you liked (or didn't like) about this recipe or draw a picture of what you made!

Food for Thought

Matter is anything that takes up space. Our whole world is made of matter—people, animals, water, air, houses, rocks, cupcakes . . . everything! Matter can exist in three different states: a **solid**, a **liquid**, or a **gas**. A **solid**, such as a grain of rice or a book, keeps its own shape as it moves from place to place. A **liquid**, such as water or maple syrup, doesn't have its own shape; it takes the shape of whatever container is holding it. A **gas**, such as air, can expand (or contract) to fit into a given space. Just about every ingredient we use in the kitchen is a solid or a liquid. Take a look at the ingredients for your Birthday Cupcakes. Which ingredients are solids and which ingredients are liquids? (Spoiler: None of the ingredients are gases!)

Solid Ingredients:

Liquid Ingredients:

SEE PAGE 130 FOR ANSWERS

Apple Crisp

SERVES 8
TOTAL TIME 1 hour and 10 minutes, plus cooling time

You can use any sweet, crisp apple, such as Honeycrisp or Braeburn, for this recipe.

Prepare Ingredients

⅔ cup (3⅓ ounces) all-purpose flour

½ cup (1½ ounces) old-fashioned rolled oats

¼ cup packed (1¾ ounces) light brown sugar

½ teaspoon ground cinnamon

5 tablespoons unsalted butter, melted and cooled

¼ cup (1¾ ounces) sugar

2 teaspoons cornstarch

⅛ teaspoon salt

2 pounds Golden Delicious apples, peeled, cored, and cut into 1-inch pieces

Gather Baking Equipment

2 bowls (1 large, 1 medium)

Rubber spatula

Fork

8-inch square baking dish

Oven mitts

Cooling rack

Start Baking!

1 Adjust oven rack to lower-middle position and heat oven to 375 degrees.

2 In medium bowl, use rubber spatula to stir together flour, oats, brown sugar, and cinnamon. Drizzle melted butter over oat mixture and toss with fork or your fingers until mixture comes together.

3 In large bowl, use rubber spatula to stir together sugar, cornstarch, and salt. Add apples to bowl with cornstarch mixture and toss to coat.

4 Use rubber spatula to scrape apple mixture into 8-inch square baking dish. Crumble oat topping into pea-size clumps and sprinkle evenly over apple mixture.

5 Place baking dish in oven. Bake until filling is bubbling around edges and topping is golden brown, about 40 minutes.

6 Use oven mitts to remove baking dish from oven and place on cooling rack (ask an adult for help). Let apple crisp cool on rack for at least 30 minutes before serving.

Food for Thought

This recipe uses Golden Delicious apples. Do you think the apple crisp would turn out differently if you used another apple variety instead?

Some apples are great for snacking, some are better for baking, and others are ideal for making apple juice or apple cider. Apples can be sweet or tart, soft or firm, large or small. We used Golden Delicious apples in this apple crisp recipe because they have a sweet flavor and they keep their shape during baking (they don't turn into applesauce!).

There are thousands of different varieties of apples. How many can you name? What is your favorite apple variety, and why?

Before starting this recipe, set aside one or two slices of Golden Delicious apple. If you have another type of apple on hand, cut it into slices as well. Take a bite of each type of apple and think about these questions.

Notes Use this space to write what you liked (or didn't like) about this recipe or draw a picture of what you made!

- How does each apple slice look? What color is the skin? The flesh?

- How would you describe the flavor of each apple? Is it sweet, tart, or somewhere in between?

- What do you notice about the texture of each apple? Is it soft, firm, or somewhere in between?

Apple 1:

Tasting Notes

Apple 2:

Tasting Notes

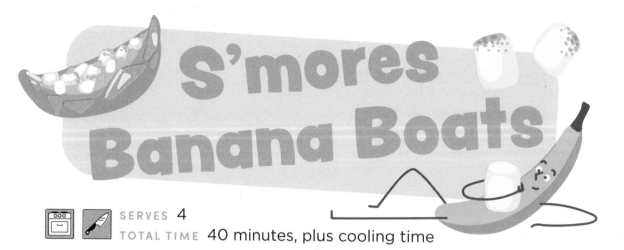

S'mores Banana Boats

SERVES 4

TOTAL TIME 40 minutes, plus cooling time

Prepare Ingredients

4 ripe bananas

½ cup (3 ounces) milk chocolate chips

¾ cup mini marshmallows

2 whole graham crackers, broken into small pieces

Gather Baking Equipment

Paring knife

Aluminum foil

Ruler

8-inch square baking dish

Oven mitts

Cooling rack

Start Baking!

1 Adjust oven rack to middle position and heat oven to 375 degrees.

2 Using tip of paring knife, slice bananas open from tip to tip, leaving peels on and making sure not to slice all the way through bananas.

3 Gently push end of banana down and toward center to open up banana into canoe shape. Place four 8-by-12-inch rectangles of aluminum foil on counter. Wrap each banana peel in foil by folding up sides of foil and pinching ends together to create canoe shape.

4 Sprinkle chocolate chips evenly inside bananas, then sprinkle marshmallows on top of chocolate chips. Transfer assembled banana boats to 8-inch square baking dish.

5 Place baking dish in oven. Bake until marshmallows are golden brown and chocolate chips have melted, 12 to 15 minutes.

6 Use oven mitts to remove baking dish from oven and place on cooling rack (ask an adult for help). Let bananas cool for 10 minutes. Sprinkle bananas with graham cracker pieces and serve.

Notes Use this space to write what you liked (or didn't like) about this recipe or draw a picture of what you made!

Food for Thought

Baking can transform an ingredient's flavor (what it tastes and smells like), its texture (what it feels like), and its appearance (what it looks like). Use this space to record your observations about some of the ingredients in these banana boats before and after they're baked. Tasting is encouraged!

	Before	After
Bananas		
Chocolate chips		
Marshmallows		

Cinnamon-Raisin Swirl Bread

 MAKES 1 loaf

TOTAL TIME 2 hours, plus 1¼ hours cooling time

Prepare Ingredients

Vegetable oil spray

2 teaspoons ground cinnamon

6 tablespoons (2⅔ ounces) plus 1 cup (7 ounces) sugar, measured separately

3 cups (15 ounces) all-purpose flour

1½ teaspoons baking soda

¾ teaspoon salt

1½ cups buttermilk

⅓ cup vegetable oil

2 large eggs

½ cup raisins

Gather Baking Equipment

8½-by-4½-inch metal loaf pan

3 bowls (1 large, 1 medium, 1 small)

Whisk

Rubber spatula

Measuring cups

1-tablespoon measuring spoon

Butter knife

Toothpick

Oven mitts

Cooling rack

Start Baking!

1 Adjust oven rack to middle position and heat oven to 325 degrees. Spray inside bottom and sides of 8½-by-4½-inch metal loaf pan with vegetable oil spray.

2 In small bowl, whisk together cinnamon and 6 tablespoons sugar. Set aside. In medium bowl, whisk together flour, baking soda, salt, and remaining 1 cup sugar.

3 In large bowl, whisk together buttermilk, oil, and eggs. Add flour mixture to buttermilk mixture and use rubber spatula to stir until just combined and no dry flour is visible. Add raisins and gently stir to combine. Do not overmix.

4 Use measuring cups to measure 1½ cups batter into greased loaf pan (use rubber spatula to level batter and scrape it out of cups). Smooth batter into even layer. Sprinkle 2 tablespoons cinnamon sugar evenly over batter. Repeat layering 2 more times with remaining batter and cinnamon sugar (for 3 of each layer total).

5 Insert butter knife into batter until tip touches bottom of loaf pan. Swirl cinnamon sugar and batter together, moving knife side to side and down length of pan. Make sure tip of knife touches pan bottom as you work. Smooth top of loaf into even layer.

6 Place loaf pan in oven. Bake until toothpick inserted in center of bread comes out clean, 1¼ hours to 1 hour and 25 minutes.

7 Use oven mitts to remove loaf pan from oven and place on cooling rack (ask an adult for help). Let bread cool in pan for 15 minutes.

8 Use oven mitts to carefully turn loaf pan on its side and remove bread from pan. Let bread cool on cooling rack for at least 1 hour before serving.

Notes Use this space to write what you liked (or didn't like) about this recipe or draw a picture of what you made!

Food for Thought

Can you turn a raisin back into a grape? Before you start your recipe, place a few raisins in a clear drinking glass and add a few inches of water. Set the glass in a place where it won't be disturbed.

Make a prediction: What do you think will happen to the raisins if they're left in the water for a few hours?

Draw a picture of a raisin before and after you soaked it in the space below.

Before   After

After at least 4 hours (or overnight), remove the raisins from the water. What do you notice? What do you think happened?

As they sat in the water, the raisins became plumper and rounder (though not as round and plump as grapes). Cut one raisin in half and see if there's water on the inside (there should be!). The skin of the raisin has very tiny holes in it. That means that tiny molecules, such as water, can pass through it.

When you put the raisins in the glass, the raisins contained less water than their surroundings. The tiny water molecules naturally moved from where there were more of them (the glass) to where there were fewer of them (inside the raisins). Scientists call this process osmosis ("oz-MOE-sis").

Almost No-Knead Bread

MAKES 1 loaf

TOTAL TIME 2 hours and 40 minutes, plus 12½ hours rising and cooling time

Prepare Ingredients

3 cups (15 ounces) all-purpose flour, plus extra for counter

2 teaspoons salt

¼ teaspoon instant or rapid-rise yeast

1 cup plus 2 tablespoons room-temperature water

1 tablespoon distilled white vinegar

Vegetable oil spray

Gather Baking Equipment

Day 1	Day 2
Large bowl	Ruler
Whisk	Parchment paper
Rubber spatula	Small Dutch oven with lid
Plastic wrap	Oven mitts
	Cooling rack
	Cutting board
	Bread knife

Start Baking!

1 **Day 1:** In large bowl, whisk together flour, salt, and yeast. Add water and vinegar. Use rubber spatula to stir and press until dough comes together and no dry flour is visible, 2 to 3 minutes.

2 Cover bowl with plastic wrap and let dough rise until bubbly and doubled in size, at least 8 hours or up to 18 hours.

3 **Day 2:** Lay 18-by-12-inch sheet of parchment paper on counter. Spray parchment lightly with vegetable oil spray. Set aside.

4 Sprinkle clean counter heavily with extra flour and then coat your hands with extra flour. Transfer dough to counter and use your floured hands to knead until smooth, about 1 minute. Move dough to clean portion of counter. Use your hands to form dough into smooth ball.

5 Transfer ball to center of greased parchment. Use parchment to lower dough into Dutch oven (let any extra parchment hang over pot edges). Cover pot with lid and let dough rise until doubled in size, 1½ to 2 hours.

6 Adjust oven rack to middle position. When dough is ready, place covered pot in cold oven. Set oven to 425 degrees and bake for 30 minutes.

7 Ask an adult to remove pot lid with oven mitts (lid will be VERY hot). Continue to bake until loaf is deep golden brown, 20 to 25 minutes.

8 Ask an adult to remove pot from oven and to carefully lift parchment and bread out of pot and transfer to cooling rack (pot will be VERY hot). Let bread cool completely on cooling rack, about 3 hours. Transfer bread to cutting board, discard parchment, slice (ask an adult for help), and serve.

Notes Use this space to write what you liked (or didn't like) about this recipe or draw a picture of what you made!

Food for Thought

Making yeast bread can feel magical: You mix together a few simple ingredients, wait awhile, and they transform into a puffy ball of dough ready to be baked into a big, golden-brown loaf. All it takes is time (and, OK, a little work). Record the transformations you observe in your Almost No-Knead Bread dough in the spaces below.

On **day 1**, after you've stirred the ingredients together, what does the dough look like and feel like? How much space does it take up in the bowl?

On **day 2**, before you take the dough out of the bowl, observe it again. What do you notice? How much space does it take up in the bowl now? What does the dough look like and feel like? How has it changed?

Discover what's been going on with your dough in "The Science of Yeast: Feed the (Microscopic) Beasts" on page 78 and "The Science of Gluten: Stretch Your Mind" on page 68.

Homemade Butter

 MAKES about ¾ cup butter

TOTAL TIME 20 minutes, plus chilling time

Prepare Ingredients

2 cups heavy cream

¼ teaspoon salt (optional)

Gather Cooking Equipment

Food processor

Fine-mesh strainer

2 bowls (1 large, 1 medium)

Airtight storage container

Start Cooking!

1 Pour cream into food processor and lock lid into place. Turn on processor and process until cream whips and turns into lumpy, liquid-y butter mixture, 2 to 4 minutes. Stop processor, remove lid, and carefully remove processor blade (ask an adult for help).

2 Place fine-mesh strainer over large bowl. Pour mixture from processor into strainer and let liquid drain away from butter lumps, about 2 minutes.

3 Use your hands to press butter lumps together to form ball. Use your hands to knead butter ball, squeezing out extra liquid. Continue to knead until very little liquid comes out when butter is squeezed, about 2 minutes.

4 Transfer butter to medium bowl and discard liquid in large bowl. Sprinkle salt (if using) over butter mixture. Use your hands to knead until combined.

5 Transfer butter to airtight storage container. Place in refrigerator until firm and chilled, about 30 minutes. Serve. (Butter can be refrigerated for up to 2 weeks.)

Notes Use this space to write what you liked (or didn't like) about this recipe or draw a picture of what you made!

Food for Thought

Cream has a bunch of (yummy!) milk fat particles swimming around in a mostly water base. Butter, on the other hand, is mostly milk fat particles stuck together in a solid mass. So how do we get the milk fat particles out of the cream? By churning cream (or processing it in the food processor), we beat air into it, which causes the fat particles to slam against each other and stick. This continues to happen, like a snowball getting bigger and bigger as it rolls, until almost all the fat in the cream is stuck together. Then, we get rid of the watery stuff left behind in the bowl and knead the butter mixture together with our hands to squeeze out extra water that's still hanging out between the fat particles. After joining the fat particles together and removing extra water, we have a substance that's more fat than water—and it happens to be delicious butter!

Try It THIS Way!

Flavored Butters: Fresh, homemade butter tastes great just as it is, or you can add ingredients to make a flavored butter. Use one of these combinations or make up your own. Fresh herbs, spices, and citrus zest are great places to start.

MAPLE-CINNAMON BUTTER

Knead in **2 tablespoons maple syrup** and **¼ teaspoon ground cinnamon** before chilling butter in step 5.

SPICY SRIRACHA BUTTER

Leave out salt. Knead in **1 to 3 teaspoons sriracha**, depending on how spicy you like things, before chilling butter in step 5.

Make It Your Way Challenge: Kitchen Sink Cookies

There are thousands of different types of cookies out there: chocolate chip, gingerbread, oatmeal-raisin, to name a few. But have you ever heard of Kitchen Sink Cookies (as in "everything but the kitchen sink!")? These cookies start with a basic dough . . . and can include almost ANYTHING else your cookie imagination comes up with!

Today your challenge is to make your OWN Kitchen Sink Cookies. You'll start with our Simple Sugar Cookies recipe on page 34 and then add flavor and texture with spices, flavored extracts, stir-ins, and press-ins. Use the ideas here for inspiration or see what you have in your pantry and refrigerator. Will you choose classic cookie components or invent your own combination? It's all up to you!

Flavorings

Add any of these flavorings along with the egg in step 3.

- Up to ½ teaspoon total of spices, such as ground cinnamon, nutmeg, ginger, cardamom, or pumpkin pie spice.
- ¼ teaspoon flavor extract, such as almond, coconut, peppermint, or orange (if using, skip the vanilla extract)
- ½ teaspoon grated lemon, lime, or orange zest

Stir-Ins

Stir up to ½ cup total into the dough in step 4.

- Chocolate chips
- Shredded coconut
- Mini marshmallows
- Chopped nuts
- Crushed potato chips
- Chopped pretzels
- Chopped cooked bacon
- Chopped dried fruit
- Oats

Press-Ins

Use ⅓ cup and distribute evenly among the 12 flattened dough balls in step 5.

- M&M'S

- Reese's Pieces

- Crushed peppermint candies

- Mini peanut butter cups

- Mini pretzels/pretzel pieces

- Crushed cookies

- Sprinkles

- Coarse or flake sea salt (use ½ teaspoon)

My Cookie Creation Draw a picture of your Kitchen Sink Cookies in the space below. Label the different flavorings, stir-ins, and/or press-ins you used.

Sketch Lots of scientists work in labs, but only a few scientists work in recipe labs—draw what you think a recipe lab looks like on this page!

FOOD FUN: AN ACTIVITY BOOK FOR YOUNG CHEFS

CHAPTER 2 Science Experiments and Activities

The Science of Pizza Dough:
GIVE IT A REST

  TOTAL TIME 30 minutes

Lots of pizza recipes (such as Cake Pan Pizza, page 28) tell you to let your pizza dough rest on the counter before you stretch it. But dough doesn't get tired, so why does it need to rest? In this experiment, you'll make two mini batches of dough. You'll stretch one right away and let the other rest before you stretch it. Does letting the dough rest make a difference?

Materials

Small bowl

¼ cup (1¼ ounces) plus ¼ cup (1¼ ounces) all-purpose flour, measured separately, plus extra for counter

5 teaspoons plus 5 teaspoons room-temperature water, measured separately

Spoon

Plastic wrap

Ruler

Vegetable oil spray

Get Started!

1 **Make a prediction:** Do you think letting dough rest will change how easy it is to stretch and shape? Why do you think so?

2 In small bowl, combine ¼ cup flour and 5 teaspoons water. Use spoon to stir and press together flour and water until shaggy dough forms, about 1 minute.

3 Sprinkle counter with extra flour. Transfer dough to counter. Use your floured hands to gather dough into loose ball and knead dough until smooth, 3 to 5 minutes.

4 Use your fingertips to shape dough into 2-inch circle and set aside on floured counter. Spray piece of plastic wrap lightly with vegetable oil spray. Cover dough with greased plastic and let rest for 15 minutes.

5 In same small bowl, repeat steps 2 and 3 with remaining ¼ cup flour and remaining 5 teaspoons water to form second dough. Use your fingertips to shape dough into 2-inch circle.

6 **Observe your results:** Use your floured hands to gently stretch second (unrested) dough into biggest circle you can, rotating dough as you stretch. When you can't make circle any bigger, place dough on counter and use ruler to measure diameter of dough (measure from 1 edge to other, across center of circle). Record your measurement, above right.

7 When first (rested) dough is ready, repeat stretching in step 6. How big a circle can you make out of the rested dough? Record your measurement, above right.

8 What else did you notice as you stretched the unrested and rested doughs into circles? Was one easier to stretch than the other? Which one?

Notes

Diameter of **Unrested** Dough

Diameter of **Rested** Dough

Use the space below to record any other observations you make.

UNDERSTANDING YOUR RESULTS

Don't read until you've finished the experiment!

Doughs made with wheat flour get their structure—and their stretchiness—from gluten. When you mix the flour with water, proteins in the flour link up and form long chains of gluten. Stirring and kneading helps the gluten become a strong network, kind of like a spider's web. The more you stir and knead the dough, the stronger the gluten network becomes.

When that gluten network first forms, it's very tight. Resting allows the gluten network to relax, which makes it easier to stretch and shape. If your dough isn't well rested, it will likely snap back when you try to stretch it, kind of like a rubber band. After just a few minutes of rest, it's much easier to stretch and shape the dough, all thanks to that relaxed gluten network. (Aren't you more stretchy when you're relaxed?)

The Science of Sugar:
THE COOKIE CHALLENGE

MAKES 24 cookies

TOTAL TIME 2 hours, plus cooling time

In this experiment, you'll bake two batches of cookies: one with brown sugar and one with white sugar. Does which sugar you use impact the cookies' flavor and texture? Do a taste test to find out!

Ingredients

Measure these ingredients TWICE. Put each ingredient in two separate bowls.

1 cup plus 2 tablespoons (5⅔ ounces) all-purpose flour

¼ teaspoon baking soda

¼ teaspoon salt

6 tablespoons unsalted butter, melted and cooled

1 large egg

1 teaspoon vanilla extract

¾ cup (4½ ounces) bittersweet or semisweet chocolate chips

Measure these ingredients ONCE.

¾ cup packed (5¼ ounces) dark brown sugar (for cookies with brown sugar)

¾ cup (5¼ ounces) white sugar (for cookies with white sugar)

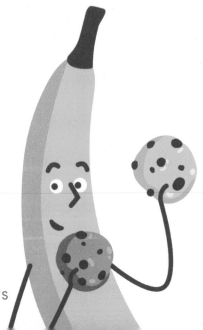

Equipment

2 rimmed baking sheets

Parchment paper

2 bowls (1 large, 1 medium)

Whisk

Rubber spatula

1-tablespoon measuring spoon

Oven mitts

2 cooling racks

Spatula

Masking tape

Marker

Get Started!

1 **Make a prediction:** Do you think the cookies made with brown sugar will taste the same as or different from the cookies made with white sugar? Why do you think so? How might they be different?

2 **Make cookies with brown sugar:** Adjust oven rack to lower-middle position and heat oven to 325 degrees. Line 2 rimmed baking sheets with parchment paper.

3 In medium bowl, whisk together flour, baking soda, and salt.

4 In large bowl, whisk brown sugar and melted butter until smooth. Add egg and vanilla and whisk until well combined.

5 Add flour mixture to sugar mixture and use rubber spatula to stir until just combined and no streaks of flour are visible. Add chocolate chips and stir until evenly combined. (If dough is really sticky, place bowl in refrigerator for 15 to 30 minutes before proceeding with step 6.)

6 Use your hands to roll dough into 12 balls (about 2 tablespoons each). Place dough balls on 1 parchment-lined baking sheet, leaving space between balls.

7 Place baking sheet in oven. Bake cookies until edges are set and beginning to brown but centers are still soft and puffy, 15 to 20 minutes.

8 Use oven mitts to remove baking sheet from oven and place on cooling rack (ask an adult for help). Let cookies cool on baking sheet for 10 minutes.

9 Use spatula to transfer cookies directly to cooling rack. Use masking tape and marker to label cooling rack "Brown Sugar."

turn the page!

10 Make cookies with white sugar:
While cookies with brown sugar are baking and cooling, repeat steps 3–9 to make cookies with white sugar, using clean bowls, whisk, and rubber spatula. (Don't forget to use white sugar in step 4!) Use masking tape and marker to label second cooling rack "White Sugar." Let cookies cool completely on cooling rack, about 30 minutes, before tasting.

11 Observe your results: Do the cookies look the same or different? Taste 1 cookie from each batch. How would you describe the flavor and texture of each cookie?

Notes Use this space to write or draw your observations from this experiment.

UNDERSTANDING YOUR RESULTS

Don't read until you've finished the experiment!

Sugar does more than make cookies sweet—it also affects their texture and their flavor. Here are some of the differences you may have noticed between your two batches of cookies.

Cookies with Brown Sugar	Cookies with White Sugar
• Darker brown color	• Lighter beige color
• Moister, chewier texture	• Drier, crispier texture
• Bend easily	• Bend a little, then snap
• Deeper, more caramelly flavor	• Milder, sweeter flavor
• Thicker and puffier	• Thinner and flatter

All sugar is hygroscopic ("high-grow-SKAH-pick"). That means it's really good at absorbing and holding on to water from its surroundings. But brown sugar is more hygroscopic than white sugar, which makes the brown sugar cookies moist and bendable, while the white sugar cookies are drier and crispier.

Brown sugar is just white sugar with molasses added to it. Molasses gives brown sugar more flavor and moisture than white sugar and that translates to chewier, more flavorful cookies. And thanks to molasses, brown sugar is also a little bit acidic. Acidic molasses reacts with the baking soda in our cookies to form bubbly carbon dioxide gas, making the brown sugar cookies a bit thicker and puffier than the white sugar cookies.

Cookie recipes can use a single kind of sugar to achieve a certain flavor or texture, or they can use white and brown sugar for the best of both worlds. The next time you make these cookies, try using ½ cup of packed dark brown sugar and ¼ cup of white sugar.

The Science of Gluten: STRETCH YOUR MIND

  TOTAL TIME 40 minutes

What is gluten, and how does it work? Find out in this flour-powered experiment. You'll make one dough with a lot of gluten and one dough with none and then STREEEEEETCH them out. You can substitute ¼ cup (1⅛ ounces) of brown rice flour for the white rice flour.

Materials

Masking tape

Marker

2 small bowls

2 spoons

¼ cup (1¼ ounces) all-purpose flour, plus extra for counter

5 teaspoons plus 5 teaspoons room-temperature water, measured separately

Plastic wrap

¼ cup (1¼ ounces) white rice flour, plus extra for counter

Get Started!

1 Use masking tape and marker to label 1 small bowl "Wheat Flour" and second small bowl "Rice Flour."

2 In bowl labeled "Wheat Flour," use spoon to stir and press together all-purpose flour and 5 teaspoons water until shaggy dough forms, about 1 minute.

3 Sprinkle counter with extra all-purpose flour. Transfer dough to counter. Use your hands to gather dough into loose ball and knead dough until smooth, 3 to 4 minutes. Shape dough into ball and wrap with plastic wrap. Return wrapped dough to bowl labeled "Wheat Flour."

4 Repeat steps 2 and 3 with rice flour and remaining 5 teaspoons water in bowl labeled "Rice Flour." Let both doughs rest for 10 minutes.

5 Make a prediction: Do you think the wheat-flour dough and the rice-flour dough will behave the same or differently when you try to pull them apart? Why do you think so?

6 After 10 minutes, unwrap ball of wheat-flour dough. Use your hands to gently pull dough apart until it breaks. Repeat with rice-flour dough.

7 Observe your results: What happened to each type of dough as you pulled it apart? Did the doughs behave the same or differently? How so? Which dough could you stretch farther?

Notes Use this space to write or draw your observations from this experiment.

STOP UNDERSTANDING YOUR RESULTS

Don't read until you've finished the experiment!

Did you find that the wheat-flour dough stretched several inches, while the rice-flour dough didn't stretch at all? Why the big difference? In a word: gluten. When wheat flour and water mix, tiny protein molecules in the flour start to link up. With time, kneading, or mixing, those linked proteins, now called gluten, form a network—kind of like a spiderweb. That gluten network is what makes wheat doughs stretchy and elastic and gives baked goods much of their texture and their shape. (See page 63 for more about gluten.)

Rice flour (made from ground-up rice) contains proteins that are different from those found in wheat flour. Rice flour's proteins don't form gluten when you add water, so the dough doesn't stretch. Rice flour is typically used to make

things like rice noodles and a sweet Japanese dessert called mochi. It's also in many gluten-free flour blends.

A strong, stretchy gluten network is what lets dough rise. As leaveners create gas bubbles in the dough, gluten traps the gas inside—like lots of tiny balloons in the dough (see page 79). The pockets of trapped gas become the air bubbles inside the finished product. Without gluten, that gas would escape and the bread wouldn't rise.

For some baked goods, such as cakes or muffins, you want only a little bit of gluten to form. Stirring the ingredients just enough to combine them creates a small amount of gluten, so the finished product will be soft and tender.

The Science of Smell: NAME THAT SPICE!

  TOTAL TIME 10 minutes

Spices are a flavorful—and fragrant—part of many baked goods. Can you identify a spice just by its smell? Round up some family and friends for a test of your senses of smell.

Materials

3 small bowls per tester

¼ teaspoon ground cinnamon per tester

¼ teaspoon ground ginger per tester

¼ teaspoon vanilla extract per tester

1 blindfold per tester

1 sheet of paper per tester

1 pen or pencil per tester

Get Started!

1 Make a prediction: Do you think you can guess a spice just by its smell?

2 Choose 1 person to organize the experiment and give out the spices. (If it's not you, stop reading here and give them the book!) In a place where testers can't see, add cinnamon to 1 small bowl per tester, ground ginger to second small bowl per tester, and vanilla to third small bowl per tester.

3 Tell the testers that they are going to smell 3 different spices. The testers' job is to see if they can guess each spice just from its smell.

4 Testers should put on their blindfolds. Hand each tester 1 small bowl of cinnamon—**do not tell them what is in the bowls!** Testers should smell their bowls, taking a few deep slow breaths in and out through their noses. Can they identify the spice? Does its smell remind them of anything? Tell testers to keep their opinions to themselves until they have smelled all 3 spices.

5 Have each tester take 3 long, deep breaths through their nose to give it a break. Repeat step 4 with bowls of ground ginger and then vanilla, reminding testers to keep their opinions to themselves for now.

6 **Observe your results:** Once all testers have finished smelling their spices, place the bowls out of sight. Have testers remove their blindfolds. Give each tester a piece of paper and a pen or pencil and have them write down what spice they thought was in each bowl.

7 Time for the big reveal! Tell testers what spice was in each sample. How many testers guessed all 3 spices correctly? Were some spices more challenging to guess than others? Which ones?

Notes Use this space to write or draw your observations from this experiment.

Even More Science

You can repeat this smell test with other ground spices, such as paprika, cumin, garam masala, chili powder, ground nutmeg, ground cloves, and more!

STOP

UNDERSTANDING YOUR RESULTS

Don't read until you've finished the experiment!

Spices come from the dried bark, roots, seeds, and fruits of plants. Many spices, such as dried cinnamon sticks and black peppercorns, are sold whole. Whole spices can be crushed and turned into powdery ground spices or combined with liquid to make extracts. **Most of a spice's flavor actually comes from its aroma (smell).** (Flavor is a combination of what we taste AND what we smell.) Our noses detect tiny aroma molecules that spices release into the air. Spices are packed with aroma molecules, which is why we're able to identify a spice just by its smell. Here are some fun facts about the spices in this experiment.

Cinnamon

Cinnamon comes from the bark on the trunk of a tropical evergreen tree. As cinnamon tree bark dries, it naturally curls into the rolled "quills" we see in cinnamon sticks.

Ginger

Ginger is a rhizome ("RYE-zome"), an underground stem of a plant that usually grows horizontally and has roots and shoots that grow out of it.

Vanilla

Vanilla comes from the seed pods of tropical vanilla orchid plants. Vanilla extract is made by chopping the pods and soaking them in a mixture of alcohol and water to pull out—or extract—their flavor and smell.

The Science of Leaveners: DOUBLE YOUR BUBBLES

  TOTAL TIME 20 minutes

Baking powder and baking soda, also known as leaveners, appear in lots of baking recipes, from pancakes to muffins to cakes. In this experiment, you'll find out how they work—and what makes the bubbliest batters.

Materials

Masking tape

Marker

4 glasses

¼ cup plus ¼ cup milk, measured separately

¼ cup plus ¼ cup buttermilk, measured separately

1 teaspoon plus 1 teaspoon baking powder, measured separately

1 teaspoon plus 1 teaspoon baking soda, measured separately

Spoon

Get Started!

1 Use masking tape and marker to make 4 labels: "Milk + Baking Powder," "Milk + Baking Soda," "Buttermilk + Baking Powder," and "Buttermilk + Baking Soda." Add 1 label to each glass.

2 **Make a prediction:** Which combination of liquid and leavener do you think will create the most bubbles? Why do you think so?

3 Add ¼ cup milk to each glass labeled "Milk." Add ¼ cup buttermilk to each glass labeled "Buttermilk."

4 Add 1 teaspoon baking powder to each glass labeled "Baking Powder." Add 1 teaspoon baking soda to each glass labeled "Baking Soda."

5 Use spoon to gently stir together mixture in each glass, cleaning spoon between glasses. Let mixtures sit for 5 minutes.

6 **Observe your results:** Which mixture created the most bubbles? Which mixture created the least?

Notes Draw what you observed in each glass below.

| Milk + Baking Soda | Milk + Baking Powder | Buttermilk + Baking Soda | Buttermilk + Baking Powder |

 STOP

UNDERSTANDING YOUR RESULTS

Don't read until you've finished the experiment!

In the America's Test Kitchen Kids lab, the glass with buttermilk and baking powder had the most bubbles after 5 minutes. The glass with milk and baking powder and the glass with buttermilk and baking soda both bubbled, too, just not quite as much. There were no bubbles in the glass with milk and baking soda.

Baking soda and baking powder are both chemical leaveners—they help baked goods rise, without the need to use yeast. Even though their names are similar and they're both used in baking recipes, they work in different ways. When baking soda comes in contact with an acid, it creates bubbles of carbon dioxide gas. Buttermilk is more acidic than plain milk, so when baking soda was added to that glass, it reacted with the buttermilk's acid to create bubbles. (See it in action in Cinnamon-Raisin Swirl Bread, page 52.)

Baking powder, on the other hand, contains an acid and it contains some baking soda, so it needs only a liquid—any liquid—to start creating carbon dioxide gas. That's why both the milk and buttermilk created bubbles when mixed with the baking powder. So for the fluffiest baked goods with the highest rise, make sure that you're adding ingredients that will create bubbles when mixed together!

The Science of Eggs: CAKE ON THE RISE

SERVES 1 to 2
TOTAL TIME 40 minutes

Find out what role eggs play in cakes—and make cake in the microwave!—in this sweet science experiment. These chocolaty cakes are best enjoyed warm. We highly recommend using Dutch-processed cocoa powder for this experiment. Natural cocoa powder will make the mug cakes drier in texture and lighter in color.

Ingredients

¼ cup (1¼ ounces) all-purpose flour

½ teaspoon baking powder

4 tablespoons unsalted butter, cut into 4 pieces

3 tablespoons semisweet chocolate chips

¼ cup (1¾ ounces) sugar

2 tablespoons Dutch-processed cocoa powder

1 teaspoon vanilla extract

⅛ teaspoon salt

1 large egg

Equipment

Masking tape

Marker

2 coffee mugs

2 bowls (1 medium microwave-safe, 1 small)

Whisk

Spoon

¼-cup dry measuring cup

Oven mitts

1 spoon per taster

Get Started!

1 Use masking tape and marker to label 1 coffee mug "Egg" and second mug "No Egg."

2 In small bowl, whisk together flour and baking powder.

3 In medium microwave-safe bowl, combine butter and chocolate chips. Heat in microwave at 50 percent power for 1 minute. Stir mixture with spoon. Heat in microwave at 50 percent power until melted, about 1 minute. Remove bowl from microwave.

4 Add sugar, cocoa, vanilla, and salt to chocolate mixture and whisk until smooth. Add flour mixture and whisk until smooth. Use ¼-cup dry measuring cup to transfer ¼ cup batter to coffee mug labeled "No Egg."

5 Add egg to remaining batter and whisk until smooth. Use spoon to transfer batter to coffee mug labeled "Egg."

6 **Make a prediction:** Do you think the cake with no egg will look the same as or different from the cake with the egg? Do you think it will taste the same or different? How so?

7 Place mugs on opposite sides of microwave turntable. Cook in microwave at 50 percent power for 1 minute. Use spoon to stir batter in each mug, making sure to reach bottom of mug.

turn the page!

8 Cook in microwave at 50 percent power for 1 minute (batter might rise to below rim of mug and cakes should look slightly wet around edges—if tops still look very wet, cook in microwave at 50 percent power for 15 to 30 seconds more). Use oven mitts to remove mugs from microwave and let cool for 5 minutes.

9 **Observe your results:** Do the cakes look the same or different? How so? Use spoons to take a taste of each cake. How would you describe the flavor and texture of each cake? Which do you like better, the version with an egg or without?

10 **Eat your experiment:** Enjoy your mug cakes on their own or top them with Whipped Cream (see page 88), fresh berries, or a scoop of ice cream. (Note: The cake without egg has a tendency to stick to the mug if it sits for too long. If you choose not to eat it, we recommend washing out the mug right away.)

Notes Draw how your cakes looked in each of the mugs below.

Egg   No Egg

UNDERSTANDING YOUR RESULTS

Don't read until you've finished the experiment!

When we tried this "eggsperiment" in the America's Test Kitchen Kids lab, the mug cake with no egg rose only a tiny bit as it baked, and it had a very dense, thick texture—it didn't taste much like the cakes we know and love. The mug cake with an egg rose all the way to the top of the mug, and its texture was lighter; fluffier; and more, well, cakey. How did yours turn out?

Eggs play a big role in giving cakes their height and their texture— even cakes that are baked in the microwave! An egg is made of about 75 percent water, plus some fat and some protein. The water in an egg is the main source of moisture in lots of cake recipes—including this one. When a cake batter with eggs bakes in a hot oven or in the microwave, its water turns to steam. That steam makes the batter grow and expand.

At the same time, the egg's proteins transform from runny liquids into sturdy solids, trapping steam inside the cake—like thousands and thousands of extremely tiny balloons. If you observe a spoonful of your mug cake with an egg up close, you'll see lots of teeny-weeny air bubbles.

The Science of Yeast: FEED THE (MICROSCOPIC) BEASTS

  TOTAL TIME 15 minutes, plus 1 to 1½ hours rising time

Did you know that yeast is alive? It's a tiny, single-celled creature—just ½ teaspoon contains millions of them. As yeast cells eat, they "burp" out carbon dioxide gas (kind of like us!), which creates all those holes inside a chewy loaf of bread. In this experiment, you'll find out what yeast likes to eat. Don't substitute active dry yeast—it won't work in this experiment.

Materials

Marker

3 snack-size zipper-lock bags

Measuring spoons

1½ teaspoons instant or rapid-rise yeast

½ teaspoon sugar

½ teaspoon salt

½ teaspoon all-purpose flour

6 tablespoons room-temperature water

Rimmed baking sheet

Get Started!

1 Use marker to label 1 zipper-lock bag "Sugar," second bag "Salt," and third bag "Flour." Add ½ teaspoon yeast to each bag.

2 Add sugar to bag labeled "Sugar." Add salt to bag labeled "Salt." Add flour to bag labeled "Flour."

3 Add 2 tablespoons water to each bag. Seal bags, squeezing out as much air as possible. Place bags on rimmed baking sheet. Set aside baking sheet in place where it won't be disturbed.

4 Make a prediction: In which bag do you think the yeast will be the MOST active (make the most carbon dioxide gas)? Why do you think so?

5 Observe your results: After 1 to 1½ hours, observe your experiment: Which bag inflated the most? Those yeast cells were the MOST active. Which bag is the flattest? Those yeast cells were the LEAST active. How do your results compare with your prediction?

Notes Use this space to write or draw your observations from this activity.

STOP

UNDERSTANDING YOUR RESULTS
Don't read until you've finished the experiment!

In the America's Test Kitchen Kids lab, we observed that the "Sugar" bag inflated the most (it was like a very full balloon!), the "Flour" bag inflated a little bit, and the "Salt" bag did not inflate at all. You could say that yeast has a sweet tooth!

The yeast cells started eating the sugar right away, which means that they also started producing carbon dioxide gas quickly, inflating the "Sugar" bag like a balloon. In the "Flour" bag, the starch molecules in the flour first had to be broken down into sugars for the yeast to eat. When flour is mixed with water, special molecules called enzymes start breaking down the long, complex starch molecules into smaller sugar molecules. Since the yeast cells had to wait a bit

for their food in the "Flour" bag, they didn't produce as much gas in the same amount of time. And while you'll find salt in lots of yeasted recipes, it's not something that yeast eats, which is why the "Salt" bag did not inflate.

In most yeasted baked goods, including our Almost No-Knead Bread (page 54), the yeast feasts on the flour in the dough, once some of it is broken down into sugar molecules. The carbon dioxide gas from the yeast's "burps" gets trapped inside the dough, which is what causes it to rise and inflate. The trapped gas is also part of what creates all those holes inside a chewy loaf of bread.

The Science of Salty and Sweet:
COOKIE EDITION

   MAKES 10 cookies
TOTAL TIME 45 minutes, plus cooling time

In this experiment (which is also a recipe) you'll bake a batch of sugar cookies. After your cookies are baked, you'll sprinkle half of them with salt and leave half plain. Then you'll taste each type of cookie and find out if the salt changes the cookies' flavor.

Ingredients

1 cup plus 1 tablespoon (5⅓ ounces) all-purpose flour

¼ teaspoon baking soda

⅛ teaspoon baking powder

¾ cup plus 2 tablespoons packed (6⅛ ounces) dark brown sugar

7 tablespoons unsalted butter, melted

1 large egg yolk

1½ teaspoons vanilla extract

¼ teaspoon coarse or flake sea salt

Equipment

Rimmed baking sheet

Parchment paper

2 bowls (1 large, 1 medium)

Whisk

Rubber spatula

1-tablespoon measuring spoon

Oven mitts

Cooling rack

Get Started!

1 Make a prediction: Do you think adding a sprinkle of salt will affect the flavor of the cookies? How so? Why do you think so?

2 Adjust oven rack to middle position and heat oven to 350 degrees. Line rimmed baking sheet with parchment paper.

3 In medium bowl, whisk together flour, baking soda, and baking powder.

4 In large bowl, whisk brown sugar and melted butter until smooth and no lumps remain, about 30 seconds. Add egg yolk and vanilla and whisk until well combined, about 30 seconds.

5 Add flour mixture to brown sugar mixture and use rubber spatula to stir until just combined and no dry flour is visible, about 1 minute.

6 Use your slightly wet hands to roll dough into 10 balls (about 2 tablespoons each). Place dough balls on parchment-lined baking sheet, leaving space between balls.

7 Place baking sheet in oven. Bake cookies until edges are beginning to set but centers are still soft and puffy (cookies will look raw between cracks and seem underdone), 15 to 20 minutes. Use oven mitts to remove baking sheet from oven and place on cooling rack (ask an adult for help).

8 Sprinkle sea salt evenly over 5 cookies. Let cookies cool completely on baking sheet, about 30 minutes.

9 **Observe your results:** Invite your family and friends to join your taste test. Have everyone take a bite of an unsalted cookie. Ask them to chew slowly and think about the flavor.

10 Have everyone take a bite of a salted cookie, again chewing slowly while they think about the flavor.

11 Ask your tasters to describe the flavor of each type of cookie. Do the salted and unsalted cookies taste the same or different? How so?

Notes Use this space to write or draw your observations from this experiment.

STOP | UNDERSTANDING YOUR RESULTS

Don't read until you've finished the experiment!

Did you think the salted cookies tasted sweeter than the unsalted cookies? Recipes for sweets—such as ice cream, cakes, and cookies—almost always use a small amount of salt. But they don't taste salty—so why include the salt?

Adding just a little salt—not enough to make something taste salty—can make food taste sweeter. When you're eating, your tastebuds send messages to your brain about the tastes they detect in your mouth. Scientists theorize that salt blocks tastebuds from tasting bitterness. And if you taste less bitterness, your brain believes what you're tasting is . . . sweeter!

You may have also noticed that the salted cookies tasted nuttier and had a caramelly flavor. Salt can also bring out other flavors in food, but scientists don't totally understand how it works. Maybe you'll be the scientist who figures it out!

The Science of Salt:
THE WIZARD OF OSMOSIS

MAKES 12 muffins
TOTAL TIME 1 hour 10 minutes, plus cooling time

Learn how to keep your zucchini muffins light and fluffy in this salty science experiment. You can use a food processor with a shredding disk to shred the zucchini instead of using a box grater, if you prefer.

Ingredients

Vegetable oil spray

1½ pounds zucchini (3 medium or 2 large)

¼ teaspoon plus 1 teaspoon salt, measured separately

1 cup (5½ ounces) whole-wheat flour

1 cup (5 ounces) all-purpose flour

1 teaspoon ground cinnamon

1 teaspoon baking powder

1 teaspoon baking soda

¼ teaspoon ground nutmeg

1 cup (7 ounces) plus 2 tablespoons sugar, measured separately

2 large eggs

¼ cup vegetable oil

1 teaspoon vanilla extract

Equipment

12-cup muffin tin

Masking tape

Marker

2 small juice glasses of equal size

Cutting board

Chef's knife

Box grater

Fine-mesh strainer

3 bowls (1 large, 1 medium, 1 small)

Rubber spatula

Dish towel

Whisk

⅓-cup dry measuring cup

Toothpick

Oven mitts

Cooling rack

Get Started!

Part 1: Conduct Your Experiment

1 Adjust oven rack to middle position and heat oven to 325 degrees. Spray 12-cup muffin tin, including top, with vegetable oil spray.

2 Use masking tape and marker to label 1 juice glass "No Salt" and second juice glass "Salt."

3 Use chef's knife to trim off ends of zucchini. Shred zucchini on large holes of box grater.

4 Set fine-mesh strainer over large bowl. Transfer half of shredded zucchini to strainer and sprinkle with ¼ teaspoon salt. Use rubber spatula to stir until combined. Let sit for 20 minutes to drain.

5 **Make a prediction:** Do you think the salted or the unsalted zucchini will release more liquid when it's squeezed? Why do you think so?

6 While salted zucchini drains, place clean dish towel on counter. Transfer remaining shredded zucchini to center of dish towel. Gather ends of towel together, twist tightly, and squeeze hard over small bowl to drain as much liquid as possible.

7 Transfer liquid in bowl to small juice glass marked "No Salt." Return squeezed zucchini to cutting board.

8 When salted zucchini is ready, transfer to now-empty dish towel and squeeze over large bowl used for draining (there will already be some liquid in bowl—keep it!). Transfer liquid in large bowl to juice glass marked "Salt."

9 **Observe your results:** Place juice glasses next to each other. Compare the amount of liquid in each glass. Which released more liquid, the unsalted zucchini or the salted zucchini? Draw what you observed on page 85.

turn the page!

Part 2: Make Your Muffins

1 In medium bowl, whisk together whole-wheat flour, all-purpose flour, cinnamon, baking powder, baking soda, nutmeg, and remaining 1 teaspoon salt.

2 In now-empty large bowl, whisk together 1 cup sugar, eggs, oil, and vanilla. Add salted and unsalted zucchini and use rubber spatula to stir until combined.

3 Add flour mixture to zucchini mixture and use rubber spatula to gently stir until just combined and no dry flour is visible. Do not overmix.

4 Spray ⅓-cup dry measuring cup with vegetable oil spray and use to divide batter evenly among muffin cups. Sprinkle remaining 2 tablespoons sugar evenly over batter in each muffin cup.

5 Place muffin tin in oven. Bake until muffins are golden brown and toothpick inserted into center of 1 muffin comes out clean, 25 to 30 minutes.

6 Use oven mitts to remove muffin tin from oven and place on cooling rack (ask an adult for help). Let muffins cool in tin for 15 minutes.

7 Using your fingertips, gently wiggle muffins to loosen from muffin tin and transfer directly to cooling rack. Let muffins cool for at least 10 minutes. Serve.

Notes Draw how much liquid wound up in each glass after you squeezed the unsalted and salted zucchini.

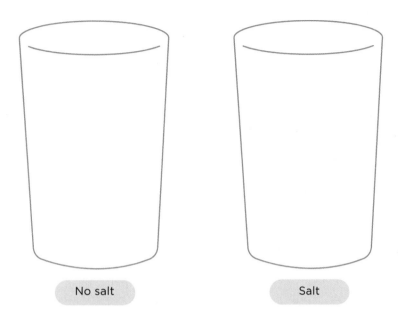

No salt   Salt

UNDERSTANDING YOUR RESULTS
Don't read until you've finished the experiment!

Vegetables and fruits such as zucchini (surprise—a zucchini is technically a fruit!) are made up mostly of water. A big challenge when you're cooking or baking with them is dealing with all that water—no one likes a watery stir-fry or a soggy muffin!

One of salt's many superpowers is that it can pull water out of food. Plants (and animals) are made up of countless tiny cells. When you sprinkle salt on plants such as zucchini, some of the water inside the cells is pulled out toward the salt. This process is called osmosis ("oz-MOE-sis").

Squeezing the shredded zucchini in a towel gets some of the water out, but salting even half the zucchini and letting osmosis do its work lets you squeeze out at least twice the amount of water. This is especially helpful when you're using zucchini, because about 95 percent of a zucchini is actually water! What happens if you don't salt any of the zucchini? You'll wind up with more water in your muffin batter, which will bake into soggy, squat muffins.

The Science of Sugar: A "BERRY" JUICY EXPERIMENT

  TOTAL TIME 45 minutes

Fruit is naturally sweet, so why do so many recipes—from fruit salad to strawberry shortcake to Apple Crisp (page 48)—call for sugar? Find out what sugar does to fruit in this juicy experiment.

Materials

Masking tape

Marker

2 small plates

Ruler

1 paper towel

Scissors

Cutting board

Paring knife

1 cup strawberries (5 ounces)

¼-cup dry measuring cup

Small bowl

1 teaspoon sugar

Spoon

1 fork per taster

Get Started!

1 Use masking tape and marker to label 1 small plate "Sugar" and second small plate "Control." (See page 9 to learn about control samples in science experiments.)

2 Use scissors to cut paper towel into two 6-inch squares. Place 1 square on each labeled plate.

3 Use paring knife to cut off leafy green parts of strawberries. Stand strawberries on cut sides and slice into ½-inch-thick pieces.

4 Use ¼-cup dry measuring cup to scoop ¼ cup sliced strawberries onto paper towel–lined plate labeled "Control."

5 Use ¼-cup dry measuring cup to scoop another ¼ cup sliced strawberries into small bowl. (Save any remaining strawberries for another use.) Add sugar to bowl and use spoon to stir until well combined. Transfer strawberry-sugar mixture to paper towel–lined plate labeled "Sugar." Set aside plates.

6 Make a prediction: Will the plates of strawberries look the same or different after 15 minutes? Why do you think so?

7 Observe your results: After 5 minutes, observe the plates of strawberries. What do you notice?

8 Repeat observing your strawberries every 5 minutes until 15 minutes have passed.

9 Use a fork to taste 1 strawberry from each plate. What do you notice about their flavor? Their texture?

10 Eat your experiment: Discard paper towels. Combine all strawberries in now-empty small bowl. Use spoon to stir until combined. Spoon strawberries over oatmeal, ice cream, waffles, or your favorite dessert (or just eat them on their own!).

Notes

Use this space to write or draw your observations from this experiment.

STOP UNDERSTANDING YOUR RESULTS

Don't read until you've finished the experiment!

In the America's Test Kitchen Kids lab, after just 5 minutes, the strawberries tossed with sugar looked moist and shiny. After 15 minutes, their juice had soaked into most of the paper towel. The control strawberries didn't change much, even after 15 minutes. They left just a small mark of juice on the paper towel. Our tasters noticed that the strawberries tossed with sugar weren't just sweeter; they were also much softer than the control strawberries. How do your observations compare with ours?

All fruits, including strawberries, are made of microscopic plant cells that are full of water. When you add sugar to fruit, the sugar pulls water from inside the fruit's cells to the outside of the fruit's cells. This process is called osmosis ("oz-MOE-sis"). That's where all the liquid on your "Sugar" paper towel came from! When cells lose a lot of water, they also become limp and soft. That's why the strawberries mixed with sugar had a softer texture than the control berries. This technique is called maceration ("mass-er-A-shun").

You might macerate fruit with sugar to make fruit salad or a juicy topping for strawberry shortcake. In other recipes, you'll toss fruits (or vegetables) with salt, which does an even better job of pulling water out of cells, before cooking or baking with them (see The Wizard of Osmosis experiment on page 82).

The Science of Whipped Cream:
WHISKED AWAY

  TOTAL TIME 20 minutes

Homemade whipped cream is delicious—but what if you don't have any cream in your refrigerator to make it? Can you use milk instead? You can substitute whipping cream for the heavy cream in this experiment, but do NOT use light cream or half-and-half. You can use a whisk to whip the cream and milk by hand; just be prepared for a workout! It will take about twice as long.

Materials

Masking tape

Marker

2 large bowls

½ cup cold heavy cream

1½ teaspoons plus 1½ teaspoons sugar, measured separately

½ teaspoon plus ½ teaspoon vanilla extract, measured separately

Electric mixer

½ cup cold whole milk

2 spoons per taster

Get Started!

1 **Make a prediction:** What do you think will happen when you whip the cream? What about when you whip the milk? Which do you think will make the fluffiest whipped cream?

2 Use masking tape and marker to label 1 large bowl "Cream" and second large bowl "Milk."

3 Add cold heavy cream, 1½ teaspoons sugar, and ½ teaspoon vanilla to bowl labeled "Cream."

4 Use electric mixer on medium-low speed to whip cream for about 1 minute. Increase speed to high and whip until cream is smooth and thick, about 1 minute. Stop mixer and lift beaters out of cream. If whipped cream clings to beaters and makes soft peaks that stand up on their own, you're done! If not, keep beating and check again in 30 seconds. Set aside bowl.

5 Clean beaters. Add cold milk, remaining 1½ teaspoons sugar, and remaining ½ teaspoon vanilla to bowl labeled "Milk."

6 Use electric mixer on medium-low speed to whip milk for about 1 minute. Increase speed to high and whip until milk is smooth and thick, about 1 minute. Stop mixer and lift beaters out of milk. If whipped milk clings to beaters and makes soft peaks that stand up on their own, you're done! If not, keep beating and check again in 30 seconds.

7 If milk has still not reached soft peaks after 3 minutes, stop whipping and continue to step 8.

8 **Observe your results:** Look at the whipped cream and the whipped milk. What do you notice? Do they look similar or different? Use 2 spoons to take a taste from each bowl. Which one would you rather have on top of your sundae or pie? Do your results match your prediction?

turn the page!

9 Eat your experiment: Use your whipped cream to top Easy Chocolate Snack Cake (page 42), Apple Crisp (page 48), or your favorite dessert. Add some chocolate syrup to your whipped milk, give it a stir, and make some bubbly chocolate milk to drink.

Notes Draw what you observed after whipping the cream and the milk in the two bowls below.

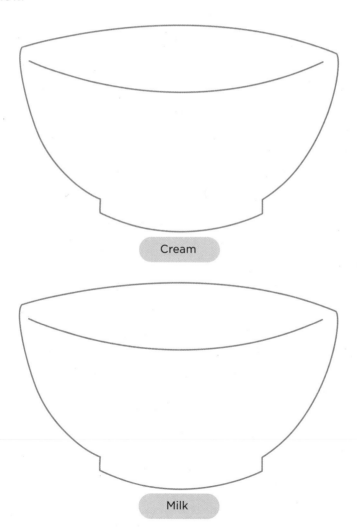

Cream

Milk

When we whipped the cold heavy cream in the America's Test Kitchen Kids lab, it turned into light, fluffy whipped cream. The cold milk, on the other hand, became bubbly, but it was still a liquid even after 3 minutes of whipping. What were your results like?

The biggest difference between heavy cream and whole milk is how much fat they contain. Heavy cream is made of 36 to 40 percent fat, while whole milk contains just over 3 percent fat. And fat is the key to making whipped cream.

Whipping cream or milk with an electric mixer (or by hand with a whisk) creates lots of tiny air bubbles. The fat in the heavy cream holds those air bubbles in place. As more and more air bubbles form, the heavy cream expands and becomes light and fluffy. Temperature is also important here—milk fat is more solid when it's cold (think about firm, solid cold butter and softer room-temperature butter). The solid fat in cold heavy cream does a great job of holding those air bubbles in place.

Milk has nowhere near enough fat to hold those bubbles in place. You can make lots of bubbles in the cold milk using your mixer, but without the fat to keep them in place they eventually pop and disappear, like when you blow bubbles into a glass of milk with a straw.

Want to use your whipped cream a little later?

Your whipped cream will keep in a bowl in the refrigerator for up to 1 hour. If you want to store it for up to 8 hours, spoon the whipped cream into a fine-mesh strainer set over a medium bowl. Place the strainer and bowl in the refrigerator until you're ready to use the whipped cream. Over time, whipped cream releases liquid. This is called "weeping." Putting the whipped cream in the fine-mesh strainer lets the liquid drain into the bowl below, which keeps your whipped cream fluffy, not watery.

The Science of Flavor: BE A CHOCOLATE DETECTIVE

  TOTAL TIME 45 minutes

Let your tastebuds play detective in this delicious taste test. See if you can tell milk chocolate and dark chocolate apart—when you can't see what you're eating! If you like, you can use chocolate bars instead of chocolate chips. Break the bars into small pieces, one piece per taster.

Materials

1 blindfold per taster

1 plate per taster

Milk chocolate chips

1 glass of water per taster

Bittersweet or semisweet chocolate chips

Get Started!

1 **Make a prediction:** Do you think milk chocolate and dark chocolate chips taste the same or different? Why do you think so?

2 Choose 1 person to give out the chocolate chips. (If it's not you, stop reading here and give them this book!) Tell tasters their job will be to taste 2 kinds of chocolate, guess what kinds of chocolate they are, and describe their flavors.

3 Tasters should put on their blindfolds. Give each taster a plate with 3 or 4 milk chocolate chips on it. Do not tell them what kind of chocolate they are tasting!

4 Tell tasters to eat the chips slowly, letting them melt in their mouths. Tasters should try to guess what kind of chocolate they are eating and think about how they might describe its flavor. (Here are possibilities: sweet, bitter, creamy, milky, nutty.) **Remind them to keep their opinions to themselves for now.**

5 Give each taster a glass of water to sip, and then repeat steps 3 and 4 with the bittersweet chocolate chips.

6 Observe your results: Once all tasters have finished tasting both types of chocolate, have them remove their blindfolds. Ask them to share what they noticed about the flavor of each chocolate sample. Do they have any guesses about the kinds of chocolate they tasted? Which did they prefer?

7 Time for the reveal! Tell tasters that the first chips were milk chocolate and the second chips were bittersweet chocolate, often called dark chocolate.

Notes Use this space to write or draw your observations from this experiment.

 STOP

UNDERSTANDING YOUR RESULTS

Don't read until you've finished the experiment!

There are two major differences between milk chocolate and bittersweet or semisweet chocolate. The first one is . . . milk! (No surprise there.) Milk gives milk chocolate its lighter brown color and mild, creamy flavor.

The other big difference is how much cacao ("ka-COW") each type of chocolate contains. Chocolate comes from the seeds of tropical cacao trees, which are called cacao beans. The cacao beans are fermented, roasted, and ground into a paste. This paste doesn't taste much like the chocolate we're used to—it's very bitter. (If you have some unsweetened baking chocolate at home, taste a little bit and see!) Chocolate manufacturers add ingredients such as vanilla, sugar, and milk solids to make the chips, bars, and candies we know and love.

Dark chocolate contains up to eight times more cacao than milk chocolate does. More cacao means deeper, more chocolaty flavor and less sweetness. Hints of different flavors in chocolate, such as a caramelly flavor or a fruity flavor, can come from the way the cacao beans are treated when they're being made into chocolate—or even from where the beans are grown!

DIY DOUGHNUT SCULPTURES

  TOTAL TIME 45 minutes, plus 3 to 5 hours drying and cooling time

Make a simple, shapeable dough and use it to create your own doughnut sculptures. Be sure to use table salt, not kosher salt, in this activity—kosher salt makes a grainy dough that is difficult to shape.

Materials

Rimmed baking sheet

Parchment paper

Large bowl

Whisk

1 cup (5 ounces) all-purpose flour, plus extra for counter

½ cup table salt

⅓ cup water, plus extra as needed

Rubber spatula

1-tablespoon measuring spoon

Oven mitts

Cooling rack

Markers (optional)

Acrylic paint (optional)

Paintbrushes (optional)

Get Started!

1 Adjust oven rack to middle position and heat oven to 200 degrees. Line rimmed baking sheet with parchment paper.

2 In large bowl, whisk together flour and salt. Add water and use rubber spatula to stir and press until no dry flour remains. (If there is still dry flour after 1 minute of stirring, add 1 tablespoon extra water and stir for 30 seconds. Repeat as needed until no dry flour is visible.)

3 Working in bowl, use your hands to knead dough until smooth, 1 to 2 minutes. Sprinkle counter lightly with flour. Remove dough from bowl and place on floured counter.

4 Divide dough into 6 to 8 pieces, depending on desired size of doughnuts. Roll each piece into smooth ball.

5 Place 1 dough ball on counter and use your hand to flatten slightly. Use your finger to poke hole in center. Use your fingers to widen hole and smooth dough into doughnut shape. Use additional dough to add "frosting," "sprinkles," or other decorations to your doughnut sculpture.

6 Repeat with remaining pieces of dough to form as many doughnut sculptures as you like. (If your dough starts to dry out while you're sculpting, return it to large bowl, add 1 tablespoon water, and knead dough until it's smooth.)

7 Place finished doughnut sculptures on parchment-lined baking sheet. Place baking sheet in oven. Bake until sculptures are dried out and hard, 3 to 5 hours, depending on size of sculptures. Ask an adult to flip your sculptures halfway through baking.

8 Use oven mitts to remove baking sheet from oven and place on cooling rack (ask an adult for help). Let sculptures cool completely, about 15 minutes.

9 Use markers and/or acrylic paint to decorate your doughnut sculptures, if desired.

Food for Thought

Want to expand your doughnut shop selection? Try these sculpting ideas for more doughnut varieties.

Cruller: Roll 2 equal pieces of dough into ropes (make sure ropes are same length). Twist ropes around each other and seal ends. Leave as is for straight cruller or join ends to make circle shape.

Honey Bun: Roll piece of dough into long rope. Coil rope to make snail shape.

Filled Doughnut: Roll piece of dough into ball and flatten slightly. If you like, use spoon or small round cookie cutter to cut "bite" out of 1 side.

Iced Doughnut: Make doughnut, following step 5, left. Use rolling pin to roll second, small piece of dough into thin circle, about same size as your doughnut. Cut small hole in middle and press edges to make them wavy, like dripping icing. Press lightly onto top of your doughnut.

Sprinkled Doughnut: Roll small piece of dough into long, very thin rope. Use butter knife to cut rope into short "sprinkles." Press sprinkles lightly onto your doughnut in random pattern.

FROST THE RAINBOW

 MAKES about 2 cups frosting

TOTAL TIME 30 minutes (plus time to make cupcakes, if making)

Transform plain white frosting into a rainbow of different colors! You can use this vanilla frosting to frost Birthday Cupcakes (page 46) or one sheet cake. Don't use salted butter here. You need a little salt to balance the sugar, but salted butter contains too much. You can use 2 cups of store-bought vanilla frosting in this activity, if desired.

Materials

16 tablespoons unsalted butter (2 sticks), cut into 16 pieces and softened

1½ tablespoons heavy cream

1½ teaspoons vanilla extract

Pinch salt

7 bowls (1 large, 6 small)

Electric mixer

2 cups confectioners' (powdered) sugar

Rubber spatula

Red, yellow, and blue food coloring

Small offset spatula or butter knife (optional)

1 recipe Birthday Cupcakes (optional) (page 46)

Get Started!

1 Place softened butter, cream, vanilla, and salt in large bowl. With electric mixer on medium-high speed, beat mixture until smooth, about 1 minute.

2 Reduce speed to medium-low and slowly add confectioners' sugar a little bit at a time. Beat until sugar is fully incorporated and mixture is smooth, about 4 minutes.

3 Increase mixer speed to medium-high and beat until frosting is light and fluffy, about 5 minutes.

4 Use rubber spatula to divide frosting evenly among 6 small bowls.

5 Add food coloring to each bowl of frosting, following table at right. Use rubber spatula to stir each bowl until well combined, cleaning spatula between colors. Write or color your results in the spaces at right.

6 Use frosting to frost Birthday Cupcakes (if using) or another cake. You can frost each cupcake a different color and create a rainbow. Or load your offset spatula with 2 colors before frosting each cupcake for an ombré effect.

Bowl	Food Coloring	What color did the frosting become?
1	3 to 5 drops red	
2	3 to 5 drops yellow	
3	3 to 5 drops blue	
4	3 to 5 drops red + 3 to 5 drops yellow	
5	3 to 5 drops yellow + 3 to 5 drops blue	
6	3 to 5 drops blue + 3 to 5 drops red	

Food for Thought

There are three primary colors—red, yellow, and blue. These colors cannot be made from other colors. When you mix two primary colors together, you get what's called a secondary color. When you made your frosting rainbow, you made all the primary and all the secondary colors.

Artists use something called a color wheel to organize and think about how colors relate to each other. In this color wheel, the three primary colors (red, yellow, and blue) are evenly spaced in the circle. Can you color in the secondary colors between each pair of primary colors?

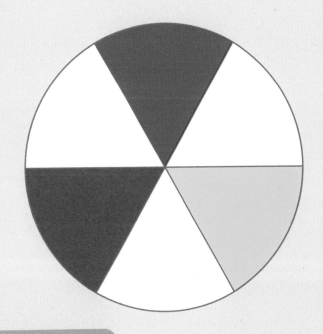

SEE PAGE 135 FOR ANSWERS

Sketch Imagine you're the chef on a mission to outer space. What do you think a kitchen would look like on your spaceship? Draw it in the space below.

CHAPTER 3 Games and Puzzles!

Pizza

There are 10 pizza-related words hidden in this puzzle. Can you find them? The words run across, down, and diagonally!

```
M  I  U  Z  A  P  L  Q  G  C  C  B  N  M  F
A  S  A  U  C  E  T  O  Y  U  N  N  Z  W  O
N  F  O  N  P  P  O  C  Z  U  W  U  C  T  D
C  N  M  H  R  P  P  N  H  F  J  B  U  G  E
H  R  Y  B  J  E  P  T  T  E  M  E  D  Q  Z
O  L  J  P  M  R  I  V  S  U  E  M  N  S  N
V  I  Y  W  V  O  N  G  L  B  E  S  X  W  O
Y  F  Q  J  T  N  G  Y  P  U  V  N  E  Z  C
G  Z  A  B  X  I  S  A  X  D  R  F  W  C  R
D  E  V  M  O  Z  Z  A  R  E  L  L  A  M  U
X  Z  N  Z  I  K  H  D  G  Y  L  D  C  S  S
E  F  F  G  P  V  D  X  B  F  L  O  P  J  T
E  O  H  A  W  A  I  I  A  N  P  U  C  I  O
I  W  C  B  D  H  Z  G  P  I  X  G  G  W  W
T  O  X  H  S  L  I  C  E  D  F  H  Q  C  Y
```

MOZZARELLA **CHEESE** **TOPPINGS**
PEPPERONI **SAUCE** **CRUST**
HAWAIIAN **SLICE** **DOUGH**
ANCHOVY

My favorite pizza topping is mushrooms. What's yours?

SEE PAGE 131 FOR ANSWERS

Cakes

This puzzle takes the cake! Can you find the 10 cakey words hidden below?
The words run across, down, and diagonally!

```
V  C  X  B  J  O  S  S  F  F  P  M  K  K  M
S  A  Y  C  I  A  O  P  C  Y  E  J  K  X  R
B  R  N  F  H  R  U  P  R  S  C  E  M  H  E
P  R  L  I  Y  J  T  F  T  I  K  J  Z  L  C
X  O  A  Q  L  F  K  H  H  Y  N  C  F  D  U
P  T  Y  S  U  L  U  Y  D  Q  Q  K  C  G  U
Z  D  E  E  Q  C  A  H  D  A  A  Q  L  L  A
B  X  R  D  U  Z  Q  Z  D  G  Y  S  C  E  L
A  T  R  E  D  V  E  L  V  E  T  B  C  L  S
T  Q  H  E  D  S  R  G  K  D  E  C  C  T  F
T  E  P  Q  U  B  F  C  C  A  N  D  L  E  T
E  Y  I  I  W  R  W  W  W  P  K  M  E  Z  R
R  X  J  E  U  E  K  K  Q  L  T  A  E  J  V
J  J  K  K  W  L  C  H  O  C  O  L  A  T  E
F  O  L  F  Z  L  F  R  O  S  T  I  N  G  C
```

CHOCOLATE   **SPRINKLES**   **CARROT**
VANILLA   **LAYER**   **FROSTING**
BATTER   **BIRTHDAY**   **CANDLE**
RED VELVET

Did you know that Boston cream pie is really a cake? It was originally baked in a pie plate.

SEE PAGE 131 FOR ANSWERS

Breakfast Baked Goods

Rise and shine! Can you find 10 breakfast treats hidden in this puzzle?
The words run across, down, and diagonally!

```
X B S O B I S C U I T K E N Y
T C A D P O B B L T E Z G I Q
B D R N S Z E E P Y W R N L
R S E O A Z Q A K A R R Z A S
A R S I I N H H E C C O F M L
B G C N E S A N Y D I L Y F D
X X O I I N S B W M A L H S S
Q O N V M Y B A R T L N G S Y
P I E D L X A B N E M M I W U
W U G U N U O R O T A X Q S L
O X U M U F F I N H H D F P H
Y H K I R G V C L Z X W D L I
L H N A S T I C K Y B U N F P
O B F S B A G E L C M T M Y Y
P F V A F T S D O U G H N U T
```

BANANA BREAD   **MUFFIN**   **DANISH**
BISCUIT   **ROLL**   **DOUGHNUT**
SCONE   **STICKY BUN**   **BAGEL**
CROISSANT

Avocado toast makes a great breakfast, too!

SEE PAGE 131 FOR ANSWERS

Baking Tools

They may be easy to find in your kitchen, but can you find the 10 baking tools hidden in this puzzle? The words run across, down, and diagonally!

```
C O O L I N G R A C K I U C B
Q M N H J V A B H A O S J L O
G U R H C I O T F X T B H G W
F F S L A M W Z S P E X K M L
R F T U Z T U C A K E P A N D
S I K N Y S P A T U L A K O U
G N Y Z T O O T H P I C K R I
P T D S D Y D R P I P W U S F
K I K J K Y V Y V K V P S T H
W N E N W Z R X O V W O U W K
H F Z P E W R C H M I X E R S
I D Z V L M M N I Y B W V L K
S T M I R A O V E N M I T T S
K G W F Q S T X X Q J K Z I O
E C R V L Z C E D D W X B Q J
```

COOLING RACK **MUFFIN TIN** **SPATULA**

CAKE PAN **BOWL** **PIE PLATE**

WHISK **TOOTHPICK** **MIXER**

OVEN MITTS

A good pair of oven mitts will protect you from burns in the kitchen. It's nice to be needed!

SEE PAGE 131 FOR ANSWERS

Baking Ingredients

Can you unscramble the letters in these jumbled words to reveal the names of 12 ingredients that are found in LOTS of baking recipes?

OLFUR   _ _ _ _ _

SGGE   _ _ _ _

LKIM   _ _ _ _

GKIABN RPDWOE   _ _ _ _ _ _ _ _ _ _ _

RUSGA   _ _ _ _ _

OLEAOCHTC SIHPC   _ _ _ _ _ _ _ _ _ _ _ _ _

ETASY   _ _ _ _ _

RTEBUT   _ _ _ _ _ _

IGKNAB DOSA   _ _ _ _ _ _ _ _ _ _

NAINNMCO   _ _ _ _ _ _ _ _

AVLLNAI   _ _ _ _ _ _ _

ACCOO WRPDEO   _ _ _ _ _ _ _ _ _ _ _

SEE PAGE 132 FOR ANSWERS

Baking Edition

Lots of baking words are prime for a rhyme! How many words can you think of that rhyme with the words below? We added some examples for inspiration.

Challenge your siblings or friends to a rhyme-off: Set a timer for 1 minute and have each person write down as many rhyming words as they can for "flour." Who thought of the most rhymes? Keep going with the remaining words.

FLOUR — Shower

BAKE — Make

PIE — Eye

EGG — Leg

KNEAD — Read

YEAST — Feast

Rise to the challenge and solve this crusty crossword puzzle.

- You don't need to solve this puzzle in order—read through all the clues and start with the ones that are easiest for you.

- It can be fun to solve crossword puzzles with friends or family (plus, more people = more brain power!).

- Finally, crossword puzzle clues are not always straightforward—don't hesitate to think outside the box.

ACROSS

2 This is hummus's best friend.

5 You might grill them during a cookout.

6 Let's "taco 'bout" a great round flatbread.

7 In a song, they cost "one-a-penny, two-a-penny."

9 Its jokes are probably pretty corny.

11 A dog treat?

12 This salty ballpark snack is a little bit twisted.

DOWN

1 This puffy roll gets its name from how it almost spills out of its tin.

3 You might find it on a breakfast plate or give one as a speech.

4 Its many small holes are sometimes called "nooks and crannies."

8 This breakfast bread's name means "crescent" in French.

10 A long, skinny loaf you might find in a picnic basket.

SEE PAGE 132 FOR ANSWERS

Trip to the Bakery

First, ask your friends or family to come up with words to fill the blank spaces in this story. Write their words in the blank spaces. Encourage everyone to be as silly and creative as they can! After you've filled in all the blanks, read the (now very silly!) story out loud.

Parts of Speech:

NOUN

A person, place, or thing (such as an anteater, playground, or grilled cheese sandwich)

PLURAL NOUN

More than one person, place, or thing (such as crackers, shoes, or rabbits)

ADJECTIVE

A word that describes a noun (such as sparkly, crispy, or tall)

VERB

A word used to describe an action (such as jump, eat, or chop)

PAST-TENSE VERB

A word used to describe an action that has already happened (such as jumped, ate, or chopped)

Mitsy's tummy _____ as she
_____**Past-Tense Verb**_____

_____ into her favorite bakery.
____**Past-Tense Verb**____

She was as hungry as a _____
_____**Adjective**

_____, but she couldn't decide what
____**Animal**____

to get!

"Hi! I can't decide between these _____
_____**Number**

things," she said to the person next to her. "I could

get a _____ bagel. Is that the one
_____**Adjective**

with _____ on top? Or, how
_____**Plural Noun**

_____ is the _____
_____**Adjective**_____**Noun**

bread this morning? Oh! That cookie looks really

_____, too."
____**Adjective**

The person looked confused. "Um, I'm not sure . . ."

they said.

"I know you can't play favorites. But if you had to

pick between the _____ velvet cake
_____**Color**

or the _____ -filled doughnuts, which would you choose?
                Noun

Or do I want an _____ bun? With the _____
                   Adjective   Noun

on top? Those are so _____ !"
                          Adjective

"I think you're mistaken . . ." the person next to Mitsy started to say.

"I get it!" Mitsy broke in. "As a baker you _____ all your
                                                    Verb

baked goods equally. Were these biscuits _____
                                                Past-Tense Verb

just this morning? I want to _____ something that is fresh
                                   Verb

out of the _____ . Do you have anything like that?"
                Noun

They tried again to respond, "For the last time, I . . ."

"Don't worry," Mitsy interrupted. "I've got it figured out. I'll take

_____ of the _____ chip cookies, three
      Number   Food Item

slices of _____ cake, half a dozen of the
              Vegetable

_____ muffins and a _____ slice of
      Food Item   Adjective

whatever pie is the freshest, please!"

"What I've been trying to tell you is that I don't work here. I'm a customer!"

said the _____ person. "The line starts over there."
              Adjective

"Oh," Mitsy said, looking embarrassed. "Well, at least now I know what

I want to order!"

You can hear more of Mitsy's adventures in our kid-friendly podcast,
Mystery Recipe! Listen wherever you get your podcasts.

Baking Mayhem!

First, ask your friends or family to come up with words to fill in the blank spaces in this story. Write their words in the blank spaces. Encourage everyone to be as silly and creative as they can! After you've filled in all the blanks, read the (now very silly) story out loud. (See page 108 for definitions of the parts of speech.)

It was a _____ Sunday morning. Mitsy tied her
         Adjective

_____ around her _____.
Piece of Clothing   **Body Part**

"Time for cookies!" she exclaimed.

"OK," she began. "Let's get the recipe out. Grandma _____'s
                                              Person in Room

_____ Cookies! The writing is a little _____,
Adjective   **Adjective**

but I guess I'll just do my best! The first step says to _____
                                                          Verb

the flour. Is that right? _____ cups, I think."
                          Number

Mitsy tried to pour flour right from the bag into her measuring cup, but it

spilled all over the _____!
                     Item in Room

"_____ _____! Oh, what a mess. That's
  Adjective   **Noun**

OK; I'll just clean that up later! Now I need to add the baking soda, salt,

_____ sugar, and . . . wait, what kind of sugar? I don't have
Color

that. I'll just add some food coloring to white sugar."

The food coloring stained her _____ and got all over
                               Body Part

the _____. But that didn't slow Mitsy down!
    Item in Room

"The next step says to add two _____ eggs. Hmmm . . .
                                Animal

All I have are _____ eggs. I don't know how to substitute
                    Animal

for those, so I guess I'll just . . . add _____."
                                              Number

"All right! I _____ the ingredients as best I could.
                  Past-Tense Verb

Now I just need to _____ the dough. Huh. That doesn't
                          Verb

sound right either. I'm not even sure how I would do that. Do I use a

_____? An electric mixer maybe?"
        Noun

Mitsy turned on the mixer, and cookie dough flew all over the room!

"Oh man, this dough is very _____. That's OK—I'm
                                    Adjective

almost done! Time to add Grandma's secret ingredient,

_____. This is going to be so good! I'll just form little
        Food Item

_____-shaped cookies here and get these
          Noun

_____ things baking. Looks like I have enough dough for
        Adjective

_____ cookies. Not quite as many as when Grandma
        Number

used to bake them, but who's counting? The final top secret recipe step is to

_____ the cookies with a _____ wash before
        Verb   **Food**

baking! It helps make them a nice _____
                                          Adjective

_____."
      Color

Mitsy put her cookies in the oven and took a look around her.

"_____!" she shouted. "I need to clean this kitchen!"
        Exclamation

You can hear more of Mitsy's adventures in our kid-friendly podcast,
Mystery Recipe! Listen wherever you get your podcasts.

Bread Around the World

Humans have been making and eating bread for a LONG time—archaeologists even discovered a burnt bread crumb that's about 14,000 years old! Around the world and in different cultures, people bake all kinds of bread, from chewy flatbreads to puffy loaves and everything in between. Find out about these far-flung bread varieties by taking our bread quiz.

1 This chewy flatbread is often enjoyed with stews and curries in its native country of India. Its spotty brown color comes from being cooked directly on the surface of a traditional oven called a tandoor.

    A. English muffin   C. Tortilla

    B. Naan   D. Injera

2 These cheesy rolls from Brazil have a crunchy crust and chewy center. They're traditionally made with tapioca starch instead of wheat flour, so they're naturally gluten-free.

    A. Pão de queijo   C. Rye

    B. Focaccia   D. Kaiser roll

3 This flatbread from China is usually fried instead of baked. It's crispy and browned, with lots of thin layers of dough flavored with a green, skinny cousin of the onion.

    A. Scallion pancake   C. Naan

    B. Pita   D. Calzone

4 This long, thin, crusty bread is an unofficial symbol of French culture. In fact, French law states that this bread must be made with only four ingredients: yeast, flour, water, and salt.

    A. Pan de mie   C. Croissant

    B. Challah   D. Baguette

5 This Mexican sweet yeasted bread is made for Día de los Muertos (Day of the Dead), a celebration of loved ones who have died. The loaves are shaped like skulls, bones, or people.

    A. Lavash   C. Pan de muerto

    B. Sandwich bread   D. Ciabatta

6 This spongy flatbread is made from a grain called teff. In Ethiopia, many dishes are served right on top of it, and people use pieces of the bread to pick up their food.

    A. Tortilla   C. Arepa

    B. Injera   D. Focaccia

SEE PAGE 132 FOR ANSWERS

Flour Facts

How much do you know about that bag of flour in your kitchen? Test your knowledge about this important ingredient by seeing if you can guess whether the following statements are true or false.

1 All flour is made from wheat.
   ☐ TRUE or ☐ FALSE

2 Whole-wheat flour gets its brown color from molasses.
   ☐ TRUE or ☐ FALSE

3 Gluten helps give bread its chewy texture.
   ☐ TRUE or ☐ FALSE

4 You can buy yeast at the supermarket, but flour also contains a tiny amount of wild yeast.
   ☐ TRUE or ☐ FALSE

5 You can make cakes and other baked goods without using any flour.
   ☐ TRUE or ☐ FALSE

6 You can make bread with just flour, water, and salt.
   ☐ TRUE or ☐ FALSE

7 Masa harina is a type of flour used to make corn tortillas, tamales, and pupusas.
   ☐ TRUE or ☐ FALSE

8 Wheat flour is made from a plant.
   ☐ TRUE or ☐ FALSE

9 All types of flour contain gluten.
   ☐ TRUE or ☐ FALSE

10 Bread, cake, and cupcake are three types of flour.
   ☐ TRUE or ☐ FALSE

SEE PAGE 133 FOR ANSWERS   GAMES AND PUZZLES!   113

In the Test Kitchen

Can you find and circle the 12 differences between these two pictures?

SEE PAGE 134 FOR ANSWERS GAMES AND PUZZLES!

A Trip to the Moon

Imagine: You've been chosen as the baker for the next expedition to the moon. The trip will be a long one, and you don't have much space to pack, so you'll have to make some tough decisions. Talk about these questions with your family or friends. Will you make the same—or different—choices?

Would you rather bring a muffin tin or a cake pan?

. . . serve only banana bread or only bagels for breakfast?

. . . bring only chocolate chips or only nuts to add to your baked goods?

. . . bring yeast or baking powder?

. . . make only pie or only cake for dessert?

. . . bring only chocolate sauce or only caramel sauce?

. . . bring only brownie ingredients or only pizza ingredients?

. . . serve hot dogs in hamburger buns or hamburgers in hot dog buns?

. . . bring an apron or an oven mitt?

. . . bring a scale or measuring cups?

You can bring only ONE color of food coloring. What will it be?

You can bring only ONE cookie cutter. What shape will it be?

You can bring the ingredients for only ONE baked good. What will it be?

Dessert Madness!

There may be no such thing as a bad dessert, but what is the BEST dessert? Use this bracket to pit these 16 desserts against each other and see which sweet treat reigns supreme. If you like, ask your family and friends to help you vote. Or have everyone fill out their own bracket and then compare your results.

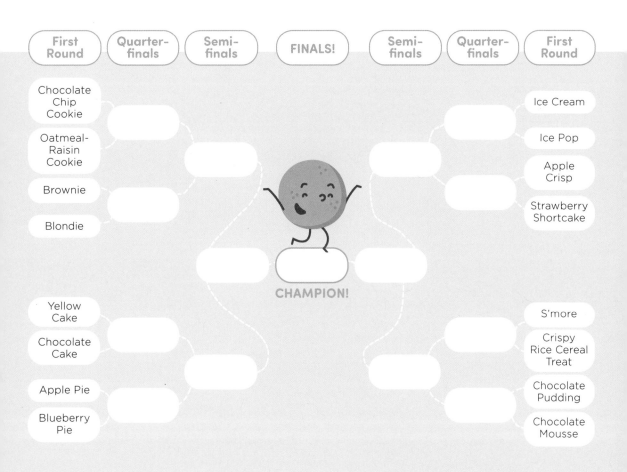

First Round | Quarter-finals | Semi-finals | FINALS! | Semi-finals | Quarter-finals | First Round

- Chocolate Chip Cookie
- Oatmeal-Raisin Cookie
- Brownie
- Blondie
- Yellow Cake
- Chocolate Cake
- Apple Pie
- Blueberry Pie

- Ice Cream
- Ice Pop
- Apple Crisp
- Strawberry Shortcake
- S'more
- Crispy Rice Cereal Treat
- Chocolate Pudding
- Chocolate Mousse

CHAMPION!

Cupcake, Fancy Pie, Croissant & Pizza

Try It!

Try It!

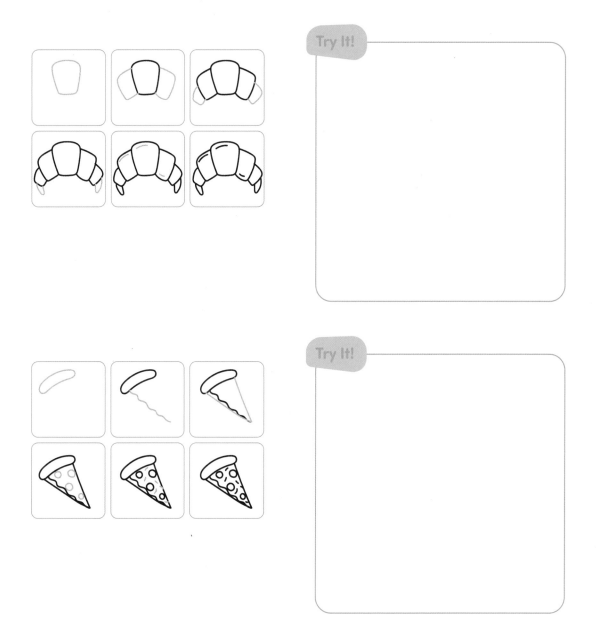

True or False?

See how well you know your way around the kitchen with this baking quiz. Play this game by yourself or with your family or friends.

1 Baking a pie with a filling that totally covers the crust is called blind baking.
   ▢ **TRUE or** ▢ **FALSE**

2 Ground spices, such as cinnamon and nutmeg, lose their flavor over time.
   ▢ **TRUE or** ▢ **FALSE**

3 The best way to melt chocolate is to cook it over high heat on the stovetop.
   ▢ **TRUE or** ▢ **FALSE**

4 Yeast dough rises the fastest at cold temperatures.
   ▢ **TRUE or** ▢ **FALSE**

5 Brown sugar is a mixture of white sugar and molasses.
   ▢ **TRUE or** ▢ **FALSE**

6 Adding a few drops of oil before whipping egg whites makes them extra-fluffy.
   ▢ **TRUE or** ▢ **FALSE**

7 Baking powder contains baking soda.
   ▢ **TRUE or** ▢ **FALSE**

8 Pound cake got its name because originally the butter was pounded to soften it before mixing.
   ▢ **TRUE or** ▢ **FALSE**

9 To make pie crust, you should have all the ingredients at room temperature.
   ▢ **TRUE or** ▢ **FALSE**

SEE PAGE 135 FOR ANSWERS

Chocolate

How much do you know about this popular dessert ingredient? Play this trivia game by yourself or with your family or friends.

1 **Cacao beans, the main ingredient in chocolate, come from a:**

A. Bush

B. Tree

C. Mine

D. Lake

2 **What are the two most common types of cocoa powder found in the supermarket?**

A. Red and black cocoa powder

B. Dutch-processed and white cocoa powder

C. White and natural cocoa powder

D. Natural and Dutch-processed cocoa powder

3 **White chocolate is made of:**

A. Cocoa butter, sugar, and milk solids

B. Cacao beans, sugar, and whole milk

C. Dark chocolate, cocoa butter, and cocoa powder

D. Milk chocolate, sugar, and milk solids

4 **Where was the chocolate chip cookie invented?**

A. Switzerland

B. Jamaica

C. France

D. United States

5 **What chocolate treat did astronauts take into space in 1982?**

A. Hot chocolate mix

B. M&M'S

C. Chocolate bar with almonds

D. Chocolate syrup

6 **What process makes chocolate shiny, hard, and less apt to melt in your hand?**

A. Humoring

B. Toning

C. Tempering

D. Settling

7 **Which type of chocolate has the most cacao?**

A. Hot chocolate

B. Milk chocolate

C. White chocolate

D. Dark chocolate

8 **How many cacao beans does it take to make 1 pound of chocolate?**

A. 10

B. 400

C. 1,000

D. 10,000

SEE PAGE 135 FOR ANSWERS

Your Dream Birthday Cake

Imagine that you could have the world's most amazing cake for your next birthday. What flavors would it be? What kind of fillings, frosting, and decorations would it have? Would it have lots of layers? Or would it be shaped like something special to you? Let your creativity flow and draw your cake below!

Give your cake a name!

DESIGN YOUR OWN Bakery

Picture this: You're a chef and you've decided to open your own bakery. What would you call it? Would it have a theme? What would you put on the menu—fancy pastries, rustic breads, sweet or savory baked goods? Use the space below to capture your creative, delicious ideas. What colors will you use on your bakery walls? Will there be tables and chairs so that people can sit and eat? What kinds of cases, shelves, baskets, or trays will you use to display the baked goods? Draw and color your ideas below.

What will you name your bakery?

Limerick

Poetry is a form of writing that makes you feel something—happy, sad, inspired, reflective—through carefully chosen words. While a lot of poems rhyme, they don't have to. The best part about writing poetry is that you can be totally free. You can write a funny poem, a love poem, or even . . . a poem about baking. Even though you can write poetry without any set structure (that's called free verse poetry), sometimes it's helpful to have some guidelines. Use this space to create your own limerick about your favorite baked goods.

A **limerick** is five lines long and is usually silly. The first, second, and fifth lines rhyme and each line contains seven to 10 syllables. The third and fourth lines also rhyme and should contain five to seven syllables. Here's an example:

My baking skills I'm trying to hone,
And my last project was blueberry scones.
They should be light and crumbly,
But I must say humbly,
That mine turned out hard, just like stones.

Try It!

. . . .

7 to 10 syllables

. . . .

7 to 10 syllables

. . . .

5 to 7 syllables

. . . .

5 to 7 syllables

. . . .

7 to 10 syllables

BAKING POETRY

Haiku

Use this page to write a haiku about a baked good that you love. A **haiku** is a traditional Japanese poem that is three lines long. The whole poem has only 17 syllables. The first and third lines both have five syllables, and the second line has seven syllables. Because they are so short, haiku poems are all about keeping it simple but powerful. Think hard about which words you choose. What are the best descriptive words you can think of? Is your haiku describing the food itself or the way a certain food makes you feel? Here's an example:

> Warm, fresh homemade bread
> Feels like a hug in food form
> Perfect for sharing

Try It!

. . . .
5 syllables

. . . .
7 syllables

. . . .
5 syllables

Acrostic

Use this page to write an acrostic poem about baking. In acrostic poems, the first letter of each line spells out a word or phrase—in this case, "baking." (On page 35, you can make an acrostic poem that spells out "cookie.") Acrostic poems have been around for thousands of years and are still popular today! Acrostic poems do not need to rhyme, and the lines can be as long or short as you like. Use the base word to ground your poem—your poem should relate to that word! You can write about baking something specific, why you like baking, what frustrates you about baking, or anything else that relates to the topic. For an extra challenge, you can try to rhyme each line. Here's an example:

> Bright and early in the morning
> All my ingredients are prepared
> Knead the dough so that it can rise
> Into the Dutch oven it goes to bake
> Now we just have to wait
> Great bread takes time to make

Try It!

B . . . .

A . . . .

K . . . .

I . . . .

N . . . .

G . . . .

Connect the Dots

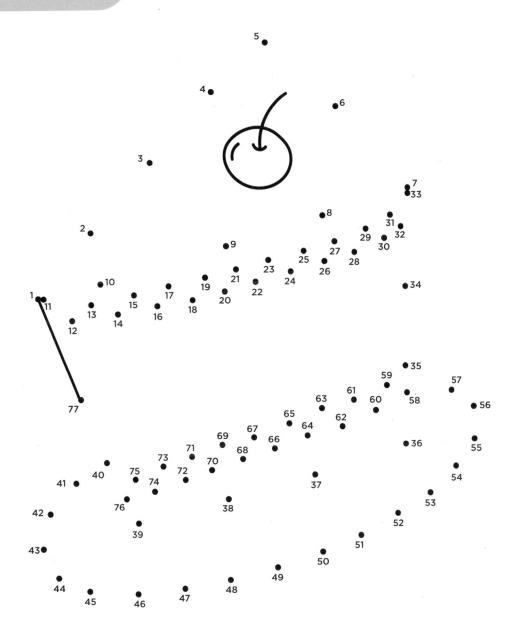

SEE PAGE 135 FOR ANSWER

Comic Strip Creator

Superheroes and comic strips go together like chocolate chips and cookies. Use the six panels below and at right to create your own baking superhero story with a beginning (first and second panels), a middle (third and fourth panels), and an end (fifth and sixth panels). Remember: A comic strip is a sequence of boxes (called panels) with drawings—and sometimes words—that tells a story (see page 29 for an example). It can be silly or serious. Every story, whether it's short or long, needs to have a beginning, a middle, and an end.

You can finish the story below about our kitchen superhero, Mitsy, or create your own comic strip about a kitchen superhero you invent! (Tip: Sketch out a rough draft of your comic strip on scrap paper before you start drawing it below!)

Mitsy the oven mitt just finished baking a batch of her famous brownies when her Danger Detector went off. Someone, somewhere was about to touch a piping-hot baking sheet with their BARE hands . . .

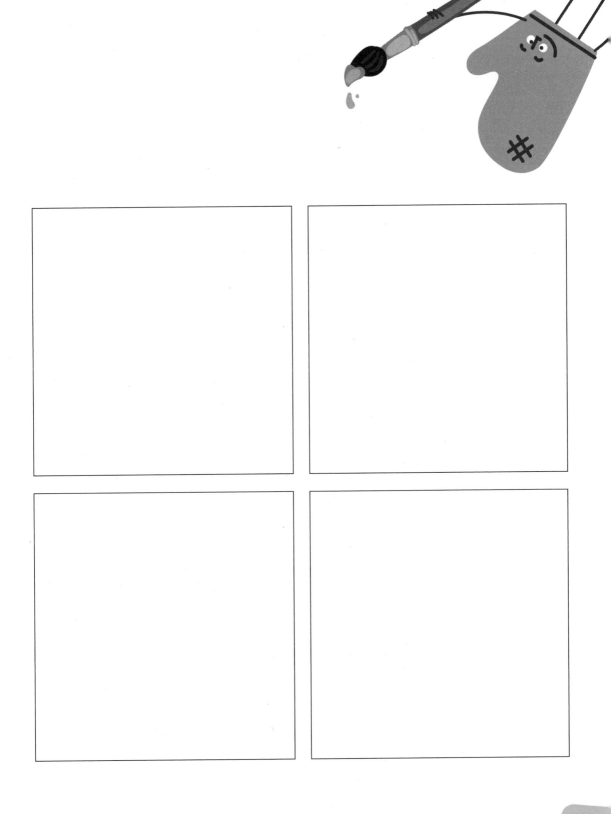

Chapter 1

CHERRY, ALMOND, AND CHOCOLATE CHIP GRANOLA

Here is the order of granola ingredient amounts, from smallest to largest:

¼ teaspoon salt

2 teaspoons vanilla extract

2 tablespoons packed light brown sugar

3 tablespoons maple syrup

¼ cup vegetable oil

½ cup semisweet chocolate chips

1 cup sliced almonds

1 cup dried cherries

2½ cups old-fashioned rolled oats

HAM AND CHEESE SLIDERS

1   2 sliders; 2 teaspoons yellow mustard

2   32 dill pickle chips

3   8 sliders; 8 slices of ham; 4 slices of cheese

SIMPLE CREAM SCONES

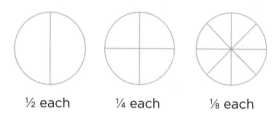

½ each   ¼ each   ⅛ each

FIRECRACKER HOT DOGS

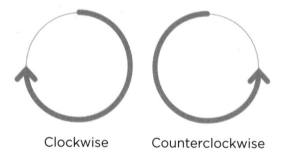

Clockwise   Counterclockwise

BLONDIES

1   8 days

2   $12.00

3   2½ cups chocolate chips

BIRTHDAY CUPCAKES

Solids: all-purpose flour, sugar, baking powder, salt, butter, eggs (whole), Vanilla Frosting

Liquids: eggs (cracked), milk, vanilla extract

Chapter 3

WORD SEARCH: PIZZA

```
M I U Z A P L Q G C C B N M F
A S A U C E T O Y U N N Z W O
N F O N P P O C Z U W U C T D
C N M H R P P N H F J B U G E
H R Y B J E P T T E M E D Q Z
O L J P M R I V S U E M N S N
V I Y W V O N G L B E S X W O
Y F Q J T N G Y P U V N E Z C
G Z A B X I S A X D R F W C R
D E V M O Z Z A R E L L A M U
X Z N Z I K H D G Y L D C S S
E F F G P V O X B F L O P J T
E O H A W A I I A N P U C I O
I W C B D H Z G P I X G G W W
T O X H S L I C E D F H Q C Y
```

WORD SEARCH: BREAKFAST BAKED GOODS

```
X B S O B I S C U I T K E N Y
T C A D P O B B L T E Z G I Q
B D R N N S Z E E P Y W R N L
R S E O A Z Q A K A R R Z A S
A R S I I N H H E C C O F M L
B G C N E S A N Y D I L Y F D
X X O I I N S B W M A L H S S
Q O N V M Y B A R T L N G S Y
P I E D L X A B N E M M I W U
W U G U N U O R O T A X Q S L
Y X U M U F F I N H H D F P H
Y H K I R G V C L Z X W D L I
L H N A S T I C K Y B U N F P
O B F S B A G E L C M T M Y Y
P F V A F T S D O U G H N U T
```

WORD SEARCH: CAKES

```
V C X B J O S S F F P M K K M
S A Y C I A O P C Y E J K X R
B R N F H R U P R S C E M H E
P R L I Y J T F T I K J Z L C
X O A Q L F K H H Y N C F D U
P T Y S U L U Y D Q Q K C G U
Z D E E Q C A H D A A Q L L A
B X R D U Z Q Z D G Y S C E L
A T R E D V E L V E T B C L S
T Q H E D S R G K D E C C T F
T E P Q U B F C C A N D L E T
E Y I I W R W W W P K M E Z R
R X J E U E K K Q L T A E J V
J J K K W L C H O C O L A T E
F O L F Z L F R O S T I N G C
```

WORD SEARCH: BAKING TOOLS

```
C O O L I N G R A C K I U C B
Q M N H J V A B H A O S J L O
G U R H C I O T F X T B H G W
F F S L A M W Z S P E X K M L
R F T U Z T U C A K E P A N D
S I K N Y S P A T U L A K O U
G N Y Z T O O T H P I C K R I
P T D S D Y D R P I P W U S F
K I K J K Y V Y V K V P S T H
W N E N W Z R X O V W O U W K
H F Z P E W R C H M I X E R S
I D Z V L M M N I Y B W V L K
S T M I R A O V E N M I T T S
K G W F Q S T X X Q J K Z I O
E C R V L Z C E D D W X B Q J
```

WORD SCRAMBLE: BAKING INGREDIENTS

FLOUR
EGGS
MILK
BAKING POWDER
SUGAR
CHOCOLATE CHIPS
YEAST
BUTTER
BAKING SODA
CINNAMON
VANILLA
COCOA POWDER

QUIZ: BREAD AROUND THE WORLD

1 **B.** Naan
2 **A.** Pão de queijo
3 **A.** Scallion pancake
4 **D.** Baguette
5 **C.** Pan de muerto
6 **B.** Injera

CROSSWORD PUZZLE: BREAD!

QUIZ: FLOUR FACTS

1 FALSE You can make flour with rice, almonds, oats, and even coconuts!

2 FALSE Whole-wheat flour is made by grinding the whole wheat berry, including the brown outer layer, called the bran. White flour is made by grinding just the inner white core, called the endosperm.

3 TRUE Gluten is a protein. It is created when flour and water mix, and it forms long strands that are kind of like stretchy rubber bands. Kneading or mixing helps the gluten strands develop into a strong network that can trap lots of air, which gives bread a nice chewy texture.

4 TRUE Wild yeast can be found in flour and will grow over time if you add water and fresh flour to it regularly. This is called a "starter" and is most commonly used to make sourdough bread.

5 TRUE Flourless cakes and other treats are popular gluten-free alternatives to traditional desserts.

6 TRUE Yeast makes bread rise; without it you can make flatbreads, which come in many forms all over the world, such as tortillas from Mexico, naan from India, and piadine from Italy.

7 TRUE Masa harina is made from dried and ground masa. Masa is ground corn that has been soaked in a special solution to help break it down.

8 TRUE The plant that wheat comes from is in the grass family. The wheat kernels (also called wheat berries) are the seeds of this plant. There are thousands of varieties of wheat grown all over the world!

9 FALSE Flours that are made with wheat, such as all-purpose flour, bread flour, and whole-wheat flour, contain gluten, but many alternative flours, such as rice flour and almond flour, do not contain gluten.

10 FALSE You'll find bread flour and cake flour at the grocery store, but not cupcake flour— that's made up!

1 The position of the oven knob
2 The number of oven racks
3 The cabinet handles
4 The flowers in the vase
5 The amount of flour in the jar
6 The number of shelf legs

7 Mitsy's eyebrows
8 Whisk's eyes
9 Which hand Orange is using to hold the cupcake
10 The icing color on one cupcake
11 The number of icing bags
12 The color of the wavy stripe on the cake

TRIVIA: TRUE OR FALSE?

1 **FALSE** Blind-baking a pie crust means baking the crust by itself, before adding the filling. It's "blind" because the crust is lined with foil and weighted down with pie weights, dry beans, or sugar to keep the crust from puffing up while it bakes.

2 **TRUE** The flavor and aroma of dried spices fade over time. Ground spices should be replaced every six months, and whole spices are good for up to a year.

3 **FALSE** Chocolate burns very easily and should be melted gently, either in the microwave at 50 percent power or in a bowl over a saucepan of simmering water on the stovetop.

4 **FALSE** Yeast works faster at warmer temperatures, which is why many recipes call for placing yeast dough in a warm place to rise.

5 **TRUE** Brown sugar is granulated white sugar with some molasses added, which makes the sugar moister and gives it flavor. Dark brown sugar has more molasses than light brown sugar.

6 **FALSE** Fat, such as oil, prevents egg whites from whipping properly.

7 **TRUE** Baking powder is a mixture of baking soda and an acid.

8 **FALSE** Pound cake got its name because it was traditionally made with 1 pound each of flour, butter, sugar, and eggs.

9 **FALSE** Using cold butter and ice water helps make pie crust that's tender and flaky.

TRIVIA: CHOCOLATE

1 **B.** Tree
2 **D.** Natural and Dutch-processed cocoa powder
3 **A.** Cocoa butter, sugar, and milk solids
4 **D.** United States
5 **B.** M&M'S
6 **C.** Tempering
7 **D.** Dark chocolate
8 **B.** 400

CONNECT THE DOTS

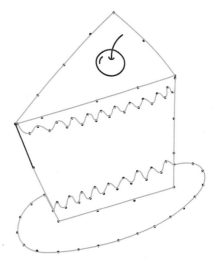

FROST THE RAINBOW

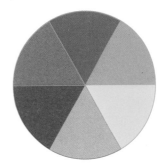

CHAPTER 5
For Grown-Ups

About This Book

Food, cooking, and baking are natural—and fun—ways for kids to learn about many subject areas, from science (biology! chemistry!) to math (fractions! measurement!) to language arts (reading comprehension! vocabulary!) to social studies (food from different regions and cultures!). They engage kids with different interests and abilities, foster creativity and problem-solving, and create a whole lot of deliciousness along the way.

Each of the kid-tested and kid-approved recipes in chapter 1 has a "Food for Thought" section. These learning moments focus on a wide range of subject areas and are designed for learners ages 8 to 13. Depending on kids' ages and abilities—and their experience in the kitchen—they may be able to tackle these recipes and learning moments on their own (or with minimal adult supervision), or they might need adult support.

Chapter 2 includes experiments and activities that highlight the many facets of science involved in baking. Kids will answer questions such as "What makes dough stretchy?," "How do baking powder and baking soda work?," and "If you can whip cream, can you also whip milk?" They'll also have hands-on fun sculpting miniature doughnuts with salt dough and custom-blending a rainbow of frosting colors.

Chapter 3 is full of educational, food-focused games, quizzes, and art-based activities. Some are designed for kids to tackle on their own, such as Word Searches (pages 100–103) and Comic Strip Creator (pages 128–129), while others are fun to play together, such as Mitsy's Silly Stories (pages 108–111) and Dessert Madness! (page 117).

Visit **ATKkids.com** for hundreds more kid-friendly recipes, experiments, activities, and quizzes to bring learning to life through food and cooking!

Food, Cooking, and STEAM

Cooking is an engaging way for kids to learn and apply STEAM content and practice STEAM skills. What is STEAM, you ask? It's more than just the vapor over a pot of boiling water; it's also an acronym for a group of highly integrated subject areas:

Science The study of the natural world and its physical properties.

Technology Anything made by humans to solve a problem or meet a need.

Engineering The process of designing solutions to problems.

Arts Activities involving skill and imagination, such as visual arts, theater, music, and dance.

Mathematics The study of numbers, operations, patterns, and shapes.

Science helps us answer questions such as "What makes bread rise?" and "What does baking soda do to cakes and cookies?" All the tools in your kitchen, from the oven to the whisk to the dish towel, are **technologies**. They've been designed by humans to solve specific problems.

Engineering results in innovative cooking tools and techniques, new or improved ingredients and recipes, and more. Baking and cooking also involve the creative **arts**, from thinking about how to decorate a cake or braid a loaf of bread to designing a piece of music inspired by a dish. And **math** is an integral part of cooking and baking: From measuring ingredients to keeping track of time to taking the temperature of food, it's nearly impossible to cook or bake without using math.

As kids work their way through this book, point out when you see them engaging in each of these STEAM subjects. So often kids (and adults) think of learning as confined to the classroom. Highlighting learning as it's happening in the kitchen allows kids to draw practical, real-world connections to what they're learning in school.

Check out Kitchen Classroom (**ATKkids.com/kitchen_classroom**) for additional ideas on how to incorporate STEAM learning into cooking and baking.

Let Kids Take the Lead in the Kitchen

As adults, our instinct is to do whatever we can to ensure that kids' projects succeed, in the kitchen and beyond. This often comes at the expense of letting kids do the work themselves. Think of yourself as their sous chef. You're there to provide encouragement and support when needed and to help with the dangerous bits, of course, but let kids do the lion's share of the tasks. You might be surprised by how much they are capable of when we adults give them the space to try on their own.

Things might not turn out perfectly (and they might not follow the instructions as carefully as you'd like), but giving kids ownership over a recipe or experiment builds their confidence in the kitchen and beyond and instills a sense of pride in their results.

Questions to Inspire Confidence
To foster kids' confidence in the kitchen, here are some questions you might ask while enjoying the (delicious) fruits of their labor.

- **You worked hard! Tell me about how you baked this. What was it like? What steps did you take?**

- **What part was the most challenging for you? How did you get through it?**

- **Would you do anything differently the next time you try this recipe? What would you change?**

These open-ended questions focus on the process of baking, not the end result. They help kids reflect on their hard work and what they learned, rather than just how their dish turned out.

One Way to Handle "I Don't Know"

If kids respond "I don't know" to all your questions, choose one question and casually respond to their "I don't know" with "If you did know, what would you say?" That simple turn of phrase—if you **did** know—frees kids from feeling as if they have to say the "right" answer and lets them say what's on their minds. Deploy this strategy strategically and sparingly—use it too often and it loses its power.

Embrace Failure

There will be times when things don't turn out the way kids had hoped—the cookies burn or the bread doesn't rise. Teaching kids how to persevere through failure and framing failure as part of the learning process helps them move into a growth mindset ("With persistence and learning, I can improve") instead of a fixed mindset ("My ability and intelligence can't change"). Remind kids that just because a recipe didn't turn out the way they expected doesn't mean they aren't a good cook—it means they are still learning. And even imperfect dishes are usually still delicious. Here are our tips for supporting kids when things don't go as planned:

- **Put a timer on sulking.** Tell kids that it's OK and understandable if they're frustrated or sad. You're going to give them 5 minutes to be upset and then you'll work with them to figure out what happened.

- **Share a time when you failed in the kitchen.** Kids don't often get to see grown-ups fail. Telling kids about your own kitchen disappointments helps normalize failure as something that happens to everyone. Emphasize that failure is part of the learning process.

- **Reflect and retrace.** Together, talk through what might have happened. Reverse engineer: Based on the outcome, what do kids think went wrong? (What could have made the cookies burn?) Walk through each step of the recipe and see if kids can identify the problem. (Was the oven too hot? Did you bake them for too long?)

- **Don't solve it for them.** Even if you know why the cookies burned (they heated the oven to 450 degrees instead of 350 degrees!), give kids space to figure it out for themselves. This small act shows kids that you believe they can overcome a challenge on their own.

- **Let kids know you believe in them.** Tell kids that you understand their disappointment but that you know they can succeed if they try again. Reiterate that you're here to support them and help them.

- **Ask if they want to try again.** Once you've talked through what went wrong, provide kids with the opportunity to try again. They don't have to immediately bake another batch of cookies, but encourage kids to use what they've learned and make another attempt in the future.

Failure and Experiments

Experiments for kids often have expected results—when you mix baking soda and an acid, carbon dioxide gas forms. But what if kids' results are different from what's expected? Reassure kids that scientists get surprising experiment results all the time. Sometimes they lead to new discoveries! Scientists also repeat their experiments to see if the same thing happens again. If time allows, have kids reread the instructions and try the experiment again. Do they get the same results? If so, spend some time together trying to figure out what they mean (see "Encourage Curiosity," below).

Encourage Curiosity

One of the most powerful things you can do for kids is model and encourage curiosity. Helping kids carefully observe their world builds observation skills and mindfulness and helps them make connections.

As you're baking and eating together, ask questions, listen to kids' responses, and share what you observe. Try using some of the prompts below.

- What do you think will happen when (　　　　　　　　　　　　　　　　)?

- What do you notice about (　　　　　　　　　　　　　　　　　　　)?

- Why do you think (　　　　　　　) happened when we (　　　　　　)?

It's OK to Not Know

Kids are naturally curious. The frequency and breadth of their questions can be astounding and sometimes overwhelming. Repeat after us: **It's OK to not know the answer to every question.** Another facet of modeling curiosity is saying, **"I don't know; let's find out."** Showing kids how to find answers, whether through research and reading or exploring the physical world, broadens their knowledge and builds their problem-solving skills.

Table Talk

Conversations around the dinner (or breakfast or lunch) table can be another opportunity for learning. As you're enjoying a meal or snack, talk about the flavors, smells, and textures of what you're eating. This not only encourages kids to eat mindfully but also provides opportunities for them to use their observation skills and broaden their vocabulary. Would You Rather? A Trip to the Moon (page 116) and Baking Poetry: Acrostic (page 126) are playful ways for the whole family to talk about food.

It's important to remember that everyone experiences food (and flavor) differently. Our food preferences are highly personal—they're influenced by our genetics and our experiences. Use these conversations as a way to celebrate differences of opinions about food. Remind kids that there isn't one "right" answer about whether something tastes good or not.

Conversation Starters

Mealtime can also be an opportunity for family conversation about food, cooking, and baking. Use the prompts below to spark discussion around the table.

- If you could open your own bakery, what would you call it? What food would you serve?

- Which is your favorite meal to eat: breakfast, lunch, or dinner? (Or dessert?) Why?

- Tell us about a time you felt proud of something you cooked or baked.

- If you could invite a character from a book to have breakfast with you, who would it be? Why did you pick them?

- Where do you think [name a food] comes from? How did it get onto our plates?

- Which do you enjoy more, baking or cooking? Why?

- Have you tried any new foods lately? What were they? Did you enjoy eating them? Why or why not?

- What was the most challenging recipe you've ever cooked or baked? What made it challenging?

- If you had a farm, what would you grow or raise on it?

- What is a recipe you haven't baked yet but that you would like to try?

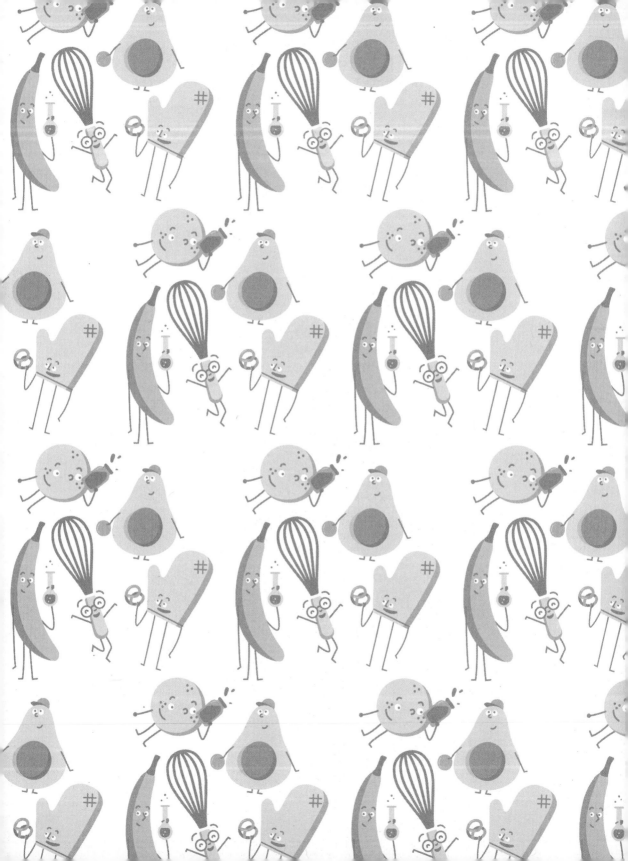